GLIMPSING
Heaven

GLIMPSING Heaven

The Stories and Science of Life After Death

Judy Bachrach

NATIONAL GEOGRAPHIC

Washington, D.C.

Published by the National Geographic Society
1145 17th Street N.W., Washington, D.C. 20036

ISBN 978-1-4262-1370-0 (hardcover)
ISBN 978-1-4262-1514-8 (paperback)

The National Geographic Society is one of the world's largest nonprofit scientific and educational organizations. Its mission is to inspire people to care about the planet. Founded in 1888, the Society is member supported and offers a community for members to get closer to explorers, connect with other members, and help make a difference. The Society reaches more than 450 million people worldwide each month through *National Geographic* and other magazines; National Geographic Channel; television documentaries; music; radio; films; books; DVDs; maps; exhibitions; live events; school publishing programs; interactive media; and merchandise. National Geographic has funded more than 10,000 scientific research, conservation, and exploration projects and supports an education program promoting geographic literacy.

For more information, visit www.nationalgeographic.com.

National Geographic Society
1145 17th Street N.W.
Washington, D.C. 20036-4688 U.S.A.

For information about special discounts for bulk purchases, please contact National Geographic Books Special Sales: ngspecsales@ngs.org

For rights or permissions inquiries, please contact National Geographic Books Subsidiary Rights: ngbookrights@ngs.org

Interior design: Katie Olsen

Printed in the United States of America

14/QGF-CML/2

For Dick and Noah and Sam

Do such moments really mean, as they seem to, that we have a life of happiness with which we only occasionally, knowingly, intersect? Do they shed such light before and after that all that has happened to us in our lives—or that we've made happen—can be dismissed?

—*Alice Munro*
"The Moon in the Orange Street Skating Rink"

CONTENTS

GLIMPSING
Heaven

INTRODUCTION

IN THE LATE '80s, I started volunteering at a neighbor-
hood hospice in Washington, D.C.—and it wasn't only
because one of my close friends, a young mother with
two children, was dying of cancer far away in California.
That was the story I told people, that I was doing it for
June, but it was half true. Maybe not even that.

The real story, the whole story is a bit simpler: I decided
to tend to the dying because I was afraid not just of death
itself (although certainly that too) but fearful of those who
were facing death and also really panicked whenever I
saw a corpse, which admittedly, hadn't been all that often.
And I thought the best way of overcoming that fear was
by confronting it—and them—twice a week every week.
Those dying patients were the future: frail, suffering, most
of them, impermanent disintegrating tenants of the only
world we knew. My therapist tells me that it was a terrible idea, confronting the thing I feared most, that fear

can only be conquered by engaging the source of terror very gradually.

But I didn't engage. I jumped in.

If you had asked me then what I thought might happen to these temporary beings after they stopped being, I would have answered flatly and with enormous assurance, as so many of those interviewed for this book once answered: Nothing. Nothing at all happens when you're dead. Your body decays, goes back to the earth, and that's about the sum of it. When I looked at the empty corpse of a former patient, dead on a hospice bed for perhaps an hour or so, I thought the same: I was gazing at a shell, something vacant and horrifying. The real person had left earlier, perhaps before my shift, and that real person was no longer.

In fact, the hospice where I first started working did ask me on a questionnaire—*What do you think happens when you die?* On the form, I tried for a perky but modulated response, one that would make me sound moderately sane:

"I have absolutely no idea what will happen when I die. But I know for a fact that someday I'll find out. Or not."

I wasn't looking forward to that day. I didn't respect death, as I now do.

I am a journalist, have been since age 22, and if there's one thing I've learned, it's not to trust anyone completely on any subject they haven't either witnessed or experienced (and even then . . .). Also, I come from a family in which death, when it was discussed, which certainly wasn't often, was generally considered a state with no options. It was what it was: the faceless all-conquering enemy. When, for example, my mother was diagnosed with Alzheimer's, which occurred some six years ago, my first question to the diagnosing physician was not *How do we handle this?*—which would have been sensible and intelligent because, trust me, it's a really hard disease to handle, and even I knew as much at the time. My question was: *How long before she dies?* Because that to me just then was the absolutely worst thing that could happen.

It was, for that matter, for my mother as well. Like her, I believed nothing was nothing. You couldn't embroider a vacuum, and those who tried, who preferred to spin elaborate gold-threaded tales about an afterlife stuffed with angels and large family reunions were simply to be pitied. As a matter of fact, if there were two elements I hoped (and hope still) never to encounter after death, it would have had to be (1) angels and (2) large family reunions.

But then I began researching this book, at the very time my mother was struggling to retain a foothold on sanity and on life. And I began contemplating the stories I heard, not simply from those who had endured death and returned, but also from those whose business it is to research, examine, and catalog such experiences. It would be easy to surmise that the approach of a close relative's death made me anxious for consolation, and maybe that's why I came to put a lot of stock in some of these experiences and also in the conclusions of the scientists who study them, but I promise you—that isn't me. Belief just isn't in my DNA.

In any case, this book has nothing to do with belief. On this subject—the issue of recollection of incidents or images or encounters that could only have occurred or been seen during clinical death—there are simply, as some of the doctors and scientists I've interviewed point out, too many experiencers and too many experiences to discount.

What you are about to read, then, are the chronicles not necessarily of what used to be called near-death experiencers, but of three categories of people: those who have actually died, however briefly; those who have observed the dead—and then, when the dead were revived, listened to their accounts of what they say occurred during that time and found them accurate; and finally, those who examine and research what we are now being told is going on after life is extinguished—the Galileos, I call them, because their voices aren't often heard, or if heard, are dismissed, their views often causing them enormous pain, the derision of colleagues, loss of tenure.

Yet their ability to examine, to listen, and to draw intelligent conclusions is really a gift of modern science. We are in the process of dissecting and reassembling the hereafter. We don't fully know what it is—yet. But we know it exists.

We are living now in what I and others like to call the age of Lazarus: Cardiopulmonary resuscitation, a frequent way of reviving the dead that was vastly improved in the

United States during the '80s, has now become so commonplace that we no longer consider it at all miraculous. But in
a way, it really is. It has opened a window, led to the resuscitation of thousands upon thousands of the formerly dead,
and brought us death anecdotes that once were the province
only of mythology or the Bible. As more and more people
have been brought back, their once stilled brains stuffed
with memories of what they say occurred while dead, there
are an increasing number of such stories. In other words,
true or false, probable or improbable, their recollection of
events they claim occurred while out tells us one important
thing: The ability to perceive and think kept on going while
they were dead. Death does not invariably signal the last
act of the play.

As I researched this book, I began to realize that however diligently a few stouthearted scientists may examine
the cases (the tens of thousands of reported cases by now)
of those who have swept through death's doors, the rejec-
tion of this field of inquiry is not simply the result of academic scorn; it is also the result of universal dread. Beyond
those doors, the landscape is assumed to be a desert—empty,
soundless, and frightening.

To the travelers themselves, of course, death valley isn't
empty at all. But the very drama of their voyages is considered suspect: no smartphone photos to show to friends,
no guidebooks or plane tickets, no elaborate descriptions
of exotic meals abroad, and most significantly, no receipts.

So what these travelers experience is a lonely voyage: exciting always, puzzling sometimes, but solitary.

And a few outside the field of death research are beginning to understand this. The other day, on my annual pilgrimage to my excellent internist, I asked her if any of her patients had been resuscitated after, say, a heart attack, and then told her stories about what occurred to them when the heart stopped.

"No, no one," she said after a small pause, but she was clearly turning the matter over in her mind. "But . . ."

"You mean they probably wouldn't have told you about it if they had seen anything striking," I prompted.

"Right, they wouldn't have," she agreed. "And it's a really interesting subject. I'm so glad you're writing about it. I believe—"

And there she cut herself off. Fast. She had other patients to see.

By then, I had met a number of physicians like my internist, approving of the subject matter, deeming it worthy of inquiry, but quiet about it. I, however, had the luxury of devoting more time to the subject. And I also believed the people I'd interviewed, a few of whom had by then become my friends. They weren't delusional or crazy, although a lot of them were concerned their old friends would think them so. They had been pretty ordinary, most of them, until their unplanned travels led them elsewhere.

So here is my question: Unlike every other possible

ending—cancer, heart disease, a gunshot wound, a fall off a ladder or a gentle slip into dementia—death happens to us all. Why isn't more research money devoted to studying what happens then? Given the mountain of anecdotal evidence, the probability that something fascinating does occur and that some of us can discuss what happened even after the brain and heart shut down, why not pour plenty of time and funding into the phenomenon and take it seriously? Especially since most of those who return to life do so with rewarding, blissful recollections.

And yet, despite these memories, so often the people who have experienced death return lonely and alone, about as lonely as the death experience researchers themselves. In the early days of my investigation, I found out just how exasperated those brave enough to examine these accounts can get when I asked Dr. Sam Parnia, one of the top researchers in the field, if the experiences reported by those who died and then returned could be caused by oxygen deficiency. Low oxygen levels and hallucinations are the common explanations among traditional scientists and other skeptics for why so many of the dead come back to life with memories. A pulmonary critical care physician and director of resuscitation research at New York's Stony Brook University School of Medicine, Dr. Parnia was swift and decisive in his response: "Your question is loaded: You don't realize it, but it's loaded. Something does happen. The first thing you have to understand is that people do have recollections of death!

"Even if some of them occurred after resuscitation, or some occurred before," Dr. Parnia continued. "Even if you took even a fraction of them to be correct, then you still have tens of thousands of people who've had them—and it's hard to brush them off. I am guided by what's been shown." These are experiences, he adds, from "people who have really died. At that point there's no brain function. I work in intensive care. People with a lack of oxygen—they don't have a near-death experience."

With so much disbelief greeting those who return from death with vivid memories, small wonder that almost none of those I spoke to, even those who had embarked on glorious voyages, recounted their strange journeys for the longest time to anyone—not spouses, relatives, lovers, or therapists—and those few who did often found their accounts discounted by those they loved and trusted most. No surprise, then, that one 2005 study determined that 65 percent of all those who return get divorced. Other researchers suggest the divorce rate is even higher.

A word of explanation before I close this introduction: The popular (but, as I and others feel, sometimes misguided and certainly ambiguous) term "near-death experience" has been dropped in this book in favor of others. Generally, I call those who went on their trips abroad "death travelers." And their experiences I refer to as "death experiences"— since there is nothing *near* about most of their voyages. Their hearts stopped beating; their brain stem activity was silent; they drowned; they were struck by lightning and needed resuscitation; they perished in hospitals, under hospice care, or in cold water. They were strangled in their beds; their breathing stopped. All that constitutes real death, not near death. If victims of such disasters recall experiences during that period of time, those are events that occurred when they were not alive.

The only instances where I use the still popular term "near death," first coined by the pioneering researcher Raymond Moody in the 1970s, is when I quote or refer to the scientist, death traveler, or physician who also uses it. It seems to be a term that, like so many of those I've interviewed for this book, refuses to die permanently.

So this is a fairly solitary voyage of discovery. I have come to know the dead far better than I ever thought, and fear them these days not at all. They walk among us, and for them, nothing is certain, because their homecomings can be so arbitrary: revived, returned, unheard, discounted, celebrated, dismissed, or applauded. It all depends on when they returned, and how lucky or unlucky they are with their relatives and friends.

This book is not just for them. It's for all of us: we the future dead, and our extraordinary future journeys.

CHAPTER ONE

THE LIGHT IS
WHAT HAPPENS

IN THE SUMMER OF 1991, Pam Reynolds Lowery, an
Atlanta songwriter, developed a numbness in her fingers and suffered a recurrence of very bad migraines.
No one exactly knew the cause of this numbness: Pam
strummed the guitar almost constantly, so that could have
been it. And the migraines might have been exacerbated by
her cigarette habit that she never could manage to shake.
But she also experienced extreme dizziness, which is why
Butch Lowery, her companion at the time, accompanied her
to a local neurologist, who, after performing a CT scan,
found the cause of these symptoms straightaway.

Inside Pam's skull, at the base of her brain, was a giant
basilar aneurysm, a weakness in the wall of a large artery
that caused it to balloon. If not remedied—and remedied
within very short order—the aneurysm would likely burst

and kill her. On the other hand, if it burst and didn't kill her, Pam was informed, she would probably be paralyzed for life. The probability of either of these eventualities occurring: 90 percent.

"So there was a choice: Do something about it, or do nothing and say your prayers," Butch Lowery tells me.

The songwriter was 35 at the time of her diagnosis, a particularly beautiful woman back then, slender and fragile. She had a cascade of sandy hair that framed a high forehead and a long, elegantly boned face. In her early 20s when her hair was shorter, brushed and waved into a golden froth, Pam looked a lot like the television star Farrah Fawcett: In fact, back then, she did a bit of modeling and also had dreams of becoming a music star.

But a decade later, those ambitions squelched, she was the mother of three young children, and after a disastrous first marriage that produced those children, was about to embark on her second marriage with Butch. Lowery, who had inherited a music publishing business from his late father, is quite open about the part he played in dampening Pam's ambitions. He did not particularly want his pretty girlfriend and future wife in the entertainment business. "It's a tough life," he tells me when we meet. "So many people want fame and fortune and I've seen too many of them go downhill." He is a large genial man of ample proportions, outgoing, garrulous, easy—and of late, quite wealthy. The house he now lives in, the one Pam selected for him, is also large and of ample proportions, its thick wood furniture diminished by the vastness of its ceilings, the breadth of its rooms. You could not imagine a more improbable husband for Pam or a more unlikely setting for her to choose. In fact, she chose it too late to enjoy it. She would never live there.

By the time of her frightening diagnosis, Pam had a number of regrets. But in one respect, she was lucky: She had Butch by her side, and he stayed by her side through everything before, during, and after her encounter with death.

I met Pam almost immediately after I embarked on this project, and like most people who come across her, I was drawn not simply to the story of how she died on an operating table and then somehow, on being revived, recalled with perfect accuracy virtually everything that had happened while dead—but to her. I was drawn to Pam. This, I was to learn months later, was not an uncommon experience. Pam was not simply beautiful. She had a husky voice, soft and quiet as a snowdrift, but each syllable was edged with an iridescent clarity. It was a perfect voice, not just for singing but also for engaging listeners, pulling them into her orbit: Family members tell me that she was a magnet for children, utter strangers too. The fact that I encountered Pam on the Internet and only on the Internet—there's a BBC interview of her speaking simply and briefly about the experience of being dead—was, I felt at the time, irrelevant.

I felt I knew her: She was that compelling. And I also knew that the odd case of Pam Reynolds Lowery is the one instance anyone knows of in which every surgical detail she recalls while dead can be—in fact, has been—checked out. A British neuropsychiatrist I spoke to calls her case "a perfect monitor" of all the anecdotal evidence suggesting that death doesn't necessarily signal a rapidly falling curtain, an instant end to the play. Her own surgeon once claimed he had 99 cases similar to hers, and no other patient had reported any experience remotely similar. The tangible evidence that Pam remembered was precise, details borne out by doctors and relatives. What I found after examining and reexamining her case, along with the people who knew her, saved her life, and loved her, is this: It was still possible to question what happened to her, but impossible to dismiss. For the rest: The voyage Pam described—the one that allowed her hints from the hereafter—that, of course, is unverifiable. For now anyway.

For a long while, I ignored Pam Reynolds Lowery, or tried to, deciding to focus instead on the recollections of people who were still alive when I met them, the stories of the still voluble. And yet, I realized, so many of them didn't compare.

In fact, as I was soon to discover, many of those who were once dead talk—now that they are alive again, accepted by fellow death travelers, and frisky—nonstop. There's no one more difficult to turn off than a person who was once dead and now isn't—possibly because for so many years many of them felt isolated, their voices stilled by the disdain of listeners, until they learned there were others just like them with similar memories of being dead. Quite a number of others, as they would eventually realize.

Those who have returned with memories call themselves "experiencers," and they generally feel there's an impenetrable division, a huge thick wall between themselves and the rest of humanity, the ones who haven't been dead, and so there are times when you love them and want to hear more, more, more but there are also times, plenty of them, when with their newly asserted freedom to speak and speak loudly, they can drive you absolutely crazy.

Pam wasn't like any of the others. There was no drama to her. Her recollections were measured and precise, bathed in the husky tranquillity of her voice. Dead or alive, I wanted to know her.

But as there was no possibility of learning of Pam's experiences from Pam herself, in February 2013, I phoned Pam's adult daughter, Michelle. On the other end of the line, there was a sharp intake of breath after I explained why I was calling. Then: "I'm not at all surprised to hear from you," said Michelle. "I've been expecting something like this lately." She seemed genuinely shaken.

So I went to Atlanta. And little by little, as Michelle spoke and Butch spoke and Pam's doctor and also her best friend and then later her cousin, I realized that there was no doubt. Pam was the only person who could begin this voyage of discovery. Her story—not just the precise scientific account of her first death, but the details of what happened after her first death—was that remarkable. And no one outside that closed circle of relatives and friends really knows to this day the extent of it.

"I met Pam when she arrived at Barrow Neurological Institute in Phoenix in August 1991, at the end of a long day," Dr. Karl A. Greene recalls. Now a Wisconsin neurosurgeon, Dr. Greene was at the time of Pam's admission a young medical resident at Barrow, four years his patient's junior and, as he puts it, "one of the lowest guys on the totem pole."

But it was precisely that relatively modest status that allowed Dr. Greene regular access to Pam: The far grander surgeon, Robert F. Spetzler, had less time to spare. Dr. Greene found his new patient "a delightful person who'd been through a lot." Like Dr. Spetzler, he'd examined Pam's cerebral arteriogram, MRI, and CT scan and knew that she had a basilar artery aneurysm that was "huge—just huge, and that an operation called cardiac standstill is one of the only ways to effectively deal with that."

Bluntly speaking, what cardiac standstill, combined with hypothermia, does is put the patient in a state of physiological death. It will be, in the best circumstances, only a temporary death. But it is, for all that, a death, lasting, in Pam's case, around an hour. The electroencephalogram (EEG) is silent during this time, as is the heart, and there is no brain stem response. Blood is drawn out of the body via a pump system, but multiple medications are infused, Dr. Greene explains, to shut down the electrical activity of the brain and prevent coagulation. There is a tube entering the mouth that extends to the lungs, a vehicle for various inhalations of anesthetic drugs that will also keep the brain asleep. Pam had been told all this before the operation.

"But what she didn't know is that that kind of operation she was about to have done is pretty uncommon for any form of brain abnormality," says Dr. Greene. He felt his job was to give her confidence in the risky but essential procedure she was to undergo.

How well the young resident succeeded in that goal is questionable. The night before the operation, Butch recalls, "We all went out to dinner—her brother, her mother, her mother's sister, and me." From her hotel room, Pam just waved them away, much to Butch's distress. "Because you know, I wanted her to talk," he says. "I wasn't sure we would ever have another chance."

But Pam was adamant. "I want to stay in this room," she told the family. "I just don't feel like talking tonight." It would be, she knew, possibly the last time she would be able to think at all.

By 7:30 the next morning, all discernible thought had ceased. Pam was lying flat out in what Dr. Greene calls "a barbiturate coma," the drugs fed through intravenous lines, and the anesthetics through the tube that snaked into her windpipe. The medical instruments were covered. Her eyes were lubricated and then carefully taped shut, and small earplugs that clicked audibly were inserted into her ears, so that doctors could monitor brain stem activity (known as "auditory evoked potentials") and tell when the electrical activity of her brain had gone flat. Pam was therefore, by the time she was wheeled into the operating room, sightless, unconscious, and deaf. Her body was cooled to 60°F; her blood, flooded with medications to prevent it from coagulating, was diverted from her body by the pump in order to give the surgeon a bloodless field in which to operate—although this was accomplished only after some difficulty.

"We have a problem, her arteries are too small," a thoracic surgeon told Dr. Spetzler. Pam's right femoral artery was of no use. The patient's left femoral artery, on the other hand, was just big enough to attach via a tube to the heart bypass pump. Then her scalp was opened, and a portion of her skull bone detached by means of a Midas Rex saw. This allowed Dr. Spetzler to remove her bone flap and expose Pam's underlying brain.

"And by that time, we had drained all the blood away from her body using the cardiac bypass pump, so we could see everything that's going on with the vascular anatomy of her brain," says Dr. Greene. "A brain aneurysm is a ballooned-out portion of a blood vessel wall—it has a neck and a dome." The way to obliterate a large basilar artery aneurysm is by placing a clip on the neck of the aneurysm, thus ensuring it can no longer fill or burst.

Next, the doctors restarted the pump, and Pam's blood resumed its usual flow through her body. Dr. Greene double-checked, peering into the surgical field with some satisfaction. "And I could see the aneurysm isn't refilling," he recalls. "At this point, the surgical team put the bone flap back into place, fixing it to the rest of Pam's skull with titanium microplates and screws. Then the heart was restarted—Pam's heart had to be shocked twice to restart it. When the procedure was finally completed, Pam had a postoperative baseline CT scan of her brain, and she went back to the recovery room. But there were so many medications still circulating inside her bloodstream that basically her brain was still not functioning."

Butch Lowery too happened to be, by coincidence, walking down that hospital corridor at the precise moment his wife was being wheeled out of surgery: She was out, he says. Totally out.

Around 12 hours later, Dr. Greene checked again on his patient. Her eyes fluttered open.

"Welcome back," said the doctor.

Pam, however, had no time for small talk. In the first place, she told Dr. Greene, she recalled quite a bit of the operation. She had managed to leave her body: "It popped out of my head," was her phrase, by which she meant Pam—the essence of Pam—could look down on that body. And then—it was as though she had a perch somewhere over Dr. Spetzler's shoulder, she explained—she could see the tops of various heads, but her vision was not like normal vision: It was focused, far clearer than ordinary vision, and Pam found herself hyperaware of everything that was going on; she saw better than she had ever seen, heard better than ever.

For example, she had imagined, been told in fact, that they were going to open her skull with a saw. Instead, the doctors wielded some odd kind of mechanical tool—it emitted an eerie high-pitched sound, "in the pitch of D," Pam recalled—and it looked not at all like a saw, but very much like an electric toothbrush. A number of blades for this instrument, she observed, were kept in a case that looked a lot like her father's old toolbox.

In the second place, Pam had been really worried during the operation: What had the doctors been doing, checking out the size of her femoral artery and poking around her thigh? They were supposed to operate on her brain!

In the third, she saw her body jump, yes actually jump, when they had to restart her heart a second time.

And finally, Pam complained, there was a song the medical staff was listening to during the operation: "Hotel California," by the Eagles, which she found really insensitive on their part, because not only does the song begin by suggesting that the so-called "hotel" might be either hell or heaven, it also contains these lyrics:

"'Relax,' said the Night Man / 'We are programmed to receive / You can check out any time you like / But you can never leave!'"

Meaning—what? Pam wanted to know. That while under the knife she would be checking out for good? That she would never leave the surgery room alive? Pam thought that surely the staff could have found a less offensive song to play.

"You know what, honey? You just need to get some rest," Dr. Greene said, trying to soothe her. "I'll be back later."

Inwardly, he was reeling. The doctor found it impossible to believe what he had just heard. The surgical saw did in fact look like an electric toothbrush; it emitted a high-pitched sound, and some of its blades were kept in what looked like a toolbox. One of Pam's femoral arteries had been too small to connect to the heart-lung machine, and there had been some discussion about that before a decision was made to try the other femoral artery. The music the doctors had played had indeed included "Hotel California." And, of course, the heart—her heart—had to be restarted twice.

She is right off the cognitive map, he kept thinking. *She was supposed to have been brain-dead.* He went straight to Dr. Spetzler, his boss, sputtering, "Pam is telling me stuff that she shouldn't know." ("Tell me what you've been smoking," a disbelieving Spetzler initially joked to his subordinate. "Because I might want some of that too!")

No one understood what happened—to this day, no one does. Peter Fenwick, a British neuropsychiatrist who, at 79, having devoted decades to death experience research, is a kind of grandfather in the field, says flatly, "My view is that when the heart stops for, say, 11 to 15 seconds, you've lost consciousness.

"Now there is no way, and I want you to put this in your book in large type—that the brain can then process information," he continues. "It can't process anything! It's got all the signs of death. No pulse. No respiration. The brain stem reflexes are gone. The brain stem reflexes come from a level in the brain that fires up the whole cortex. So if the brain stem isn't working, that means the cortex can't function." And if the cortex cannot function, that means all ability to think and all action should disappear. The person thus afflicted, in other words, is a shell, empty of what makes us human.

Butch Lowery too was astonished when he appeared by Pam's bedside, but not simply because she could provide him with details of an operation she couldn't possibly have witnessed. "I was the most aware that I've ever been in my life," Pam told him. "And I was then looking at my body and I knew that it was my body, but I didn't care."

Over the next days, Butch spoke with Dr. Spetzler about his wife's ability to recite events she shouldn't have been able to see or hear, and naturally he was stunned by the surgeon's account. In fact, although initially dubious (Butch thought at first that perhaps his wife had simply hallucinated because of the drugs administered, as one might in a dentist's chair), he was now convinced. His wife had had a death experience.

"I don't know what else it could be!" he says these days. "After listening to Dr. Spetzler, I thought, well something was there. Something did happen—there's absolutely no doubt. I had to listen to Dr. Spetzler because he is the surgeon who's doing all this. He's done this before. And he's talking about all these things—that there's no way she could have seen or heard these conversations. He's got to know."

But it wasn't simply Pam's recollection of operating room procedures and her detailed descriptions of surgical tools she couldn't have seen that amazed Butch Lowery. It was the rest of Pam's recitation of what occurred while she was under anesthesia.

As it turned out, Pam told her husband, there were other, more evocative and joyful elements to her experience: She had, she said, after a time "popped out" of her own frame, toward a shower of light that kept pulling her away from the operation itself and her own bruised, embattled body that she felt was no longer of use or any interest to her. Everything about her new environment was especially vivid, realer than real. The light she saw seemed to pour out from the end of a vortex, and she went toward it of her own free will. "It was like *The Wizard of Oz*," Pam decided, except she wasn't spinning around in the vortex of a tornado somewhere in Kansas. In fact, she saw any number of relatives and felt somehow they were all looking after her.

Within that light was a beloved uncle, Gene Saxon, who had years earlier taught her to play the guitar. Uncle Gene was 39 when he died, a big fan of pretty southern women and assorted bars. Pam had loved him dearly.

And she also heard the words of her long-dead grandmother, Grandmother Marie (whom everyone in the family called "Rie")—who had married at least seven times, maybe more. Rie was a wild woman in her day, and Pam adored her as well. She felt Rie would have certain answers, explanations to offer about her new surroundings.

"I asked my grandmother if the light was God," Pam recalled. Rie laughed at the suggestion. "Oh no, Baby," said Rie. "God is not the light. The light is what happens when God breathes." She knew then, Pam would say later, that she was standing in the breath of God.

Everything about the light seemed so compelling, so warm and desirable, that the only urge Pam had at that moment was to move ever onward, jettisoning all connection with the messy doings and high-pitched sounds of the operating theater. But Rie, once again, intruded.

"What about your children?" the old lady asked. Back then, Pam's youngest, Michelle, was just eight years old. The other two were barely older.

Pam didn't care. "You know, I think the children are going to be fine."

But her long-dead relatives, Pam told her husband, were adamant. She could not stay in the light with them.

"Go into that light and you will change," she was warned. "You will never be able to return to your body."

And with that—without a moment's warning—her Uncle Gene gave Pam a big shove. She saw her bloodied body, the one on the operating table bathed in a cold bright light, actually shudder as she reluctantly slipped back into it. It was barely her body at all. "It looked like what it was: dead . . . like a train wreck," she would explain some years later, and she was frightened at the prospect of resuming life within it. She didn't even want to look at it.

"It was like jumping into a cold pool," she later told friends. When she regained consciousness hours later, she found herself still on the respirator. This was the frigid light she was forced to return to. She had no choice.

Like it or not, she had to live.

"She told me when I was young—and it upset me—she said, 'I want to go now,'" Pam's daughter, Michelle, tells me about life with her mother after the standstill operation. Michelle is 31, just four years younger than her mother at the time the brain aneurysm was clipped, and so she understands things about Pam a little bit better now. But only a little bit.

"And I said, 'Mom, if you go now—what about us?'" Michelle continues.

At that, Pam pulled herself short. "Well no, not right now," she admitted. But wherever it was she had gone during her aneurysm operation, she added, "It's just such a beautiful place, and so good." It was one thing Pam insisted on to all her children: Death was nothing to fear. She had a name for her experience at Barrow when the doctors shut down her brain and cut open her skull. She called it The Knowing.

Pam had never been particularly driven, single-minded, or tenacious in her faith. Her father had taught religion while the family was still living in the small town that was Pam's birthplace—Kosciusko, Mississippi (also the home of Oprah Winfrey)—but after her mother divorced and remarried, Pam had been raised Mormon in Atlanta. None of these influences, however, seem to have swayed her, or at least not completely. Buddhism, Hinduism—she was interested in all of it. "She read the Torah, and she could speak with considerable knowledge about Judaism," her best friend Pam Henderson tells me. "I wouldn't call what she was religious, but she was very spiritual."

However, after what Pam would always call The Knowing, certain strong changes within her of a different nature were detectable. "She was more sensitive after the surgery—we were never allowed, never able, to be normal kids or teenagers; we were never able to lie because she always knew," Michelle explains. "We couldn't sneak out of the house at night because she knew, just knew."

What exactly did Pam know?

"There was an incident where we were in the grocery store, we're in line," her daughter recalls. Her mother hugged someone, some woman she didn't even know, and the stranger "started sobbing—uncontrollably," Michelle recalls.

"I don't know what my mother said to this woman, but she knew. This woman was having some sort of hardship, and Mom knew." Michelle thinks about that for a moment. "And Mom knew," she repeats at the end of that moment.

And didn't this hugging incident embarrass her daughter? I ask. Because I wonder about the effects on a teenager, which is what Michelle was at the time of that supermarket encounter, of such an embrace, such an intimate knowledge of a stranger's dilemma.

"Well, of course it embarrassed me! It was very embarrassing. But it was Mom. She knew a lot of things about other people."

She knew, for instance, her daughter continues, where Michelle's school friend had left a purse—and there was no empirical way for Pam to know this, because that purse was at the bottom of yet another girl's hall closet under some coats. She knew—it is Pam's best friend who tells me this story—that a teenage boy who was in a coma in the ICU of the Phoenix hospital where both were patients would, in fact, recover. It was Pam who walked up to the still body on the bed, whispering in the boy's ear: "I don't know about you, but I want to call the pizza dude and get some slices, because I hate this food here." And the boy woke up and smiled.

She knew that still another young boy (this one having drowned, then having been resuscitated—but not before breathing in a lot of chlorinated water that burned his lungs) would also recover. It was her cousin Joe Smith who asked Pam to go to the Savannah hospital where the child was. "I saw his mother," Smith recalls. "I said, 'Would it be OK, if you don't mind, my cousin has come in to see him because she might be able to do something for him.'

"And Pam held his hand, and she told him to wake up. And he did. The boy woke up 15 minutes after we left. He is fine. He is healed."

However, that drive from Atlanta to Savannah was one of Pam's very rare excursions a few years after her operation. Even the prospect of the smallest, most mundane ventures outdoors perturbed her, and as her husband puts it, "We just kind of quit going out." Pam couldn't bear leaving the house because, as her daughter Michelle tells me, "She could feel what other people were thinking; she could feel their emotions."

"So she became a recluse," Pam Henderson says flatly. She was Pam Reynolds Lowery's close friend, and the two were inseparable. "She tried to hide that from people, the people she knew well. But the people she saw on the streets really gave her the creeps. She knew what they were thinking."

What were these strangers thinking? I want to know.

"I'd rather not say," Pam Henderson replies. "But it was giving her the creeps."

All this heightened sensitivity to the concerns and thoughts of total strangers is not, as I would swiftly learn, uncommon among those who say they have memories of incidents that occurred while they were dead. There are evidently long-term consequences to the experience, some salutary, others not at all. A fair number of those who return from death, as I was soon to discover, lay claims to abilities unavailable to most of the rest of us. The only question I had when I was investigating what had happened to Pam Reynolds Lowery is this: Are these extraordinary abilities simply fantasies? A kind of self-administered blue ribbon for having died, however briefly? A result of inadvertent cerebral assaults to the brain that might have taken place before or during her standstill operation? Or is this heightened sensitivity something we have to take seriously and consider as part of the experience itself?

In fact, Pam Reynolds Lowery had incurred cerebral assaults—and more than once. I am astonished to discover from her family, because none of the literature on her mentions this, nor does the British television video clip, that maybe two weeks after that first basilar aneurysm operation, she underwent yet another in which a lesser aneurysm was clipped. It was in recovery after that second surgery that she suffered a stroke, a small one.

"She did not want this to be the focus of any experience she had," her best friend Pam Henderson tells me. "She had a stroke and came out unscathed. She just walked off the plane, no wheelchair, when she returned from Phoenix. I know because I picked her up at the airport."

But perhaps "unscathed" is not wholly accurate. Dr. Greene tells me that although Pam made a magnificent recovery from that stroke, she did need to undergo speech therapy prior to leaving the hospital.

Nonetheless, for five good years, her family was very happy to resume life with a healthier if mostly reclusive Pam: vertigo gone, fingers sentient, migraines evaporated, her thoughts expressed with the same gentle lucidity that had always characterized them. By 1996, however, the dizziness returned, as did the migraines, and she felt she had to stop driving. "We made a couple of trips back to Arizona to see the doctors, but they couldn't find anything neurological, they couldn't pinpoint anything," Butch recalls. "They tried different medications, but she just never came back to being the way she was."

By that time, too, Pam had developed chronic obstructive pulmonary disease (COPD), a progressive and usually fatal disease that makes breathing difficult and is often caused by smoking. On the rare occasions when she did emerge from the house, says her daughter, "She would approach so many people and just whisper things in their ears, and I remember thinking, *These people think my mother is a weirdo!*"[1]

But those who knew Pam, her daughter included, believed nothing of the sort. The thoughts and emotions of complete strangers, the private, silent feelings that invaded her mind and sometimes disgusted her, sometimes pained her and drove her to distraction—these became terrible burdens and they sickened Pam as much as any of her other afflictions. In his twice-yearly phone calls with his former patient, Dr. Greene heard about all of it, and he sympathized.

"Perhaps that's one reason her migraines returned," he postulates.

"I mean her filter was gone," the doctor continues. "You see what Pam experienced—it was a double-edged sword. A blessing and a curse. There were things that forever changed her, and she was overwhelmed. She was suffering spiritually because she didn't know what to do with it all. I got the sense it was hard."

A pause. "Maybe it's because I come from a spiritual background," says Dr. Greene, both of whose grandfathers were Baptist ministers, "but I used to pray for Pam."

Toward the end of her life, Pam was pretty much confined to a wheelchair, thanks to the vertigo and the hard time she had catching her breath. She grew depressed, and not simply because of the isolation imposed by illness and fragility. She was, she felt, practically alone in her intuitive abilities, in her conscious return from medically imposed death.

Where once Pam had dressed in bright, bold colors, on her return from the hospital, she wore just brown and gray. All her vanity had evaporated along with pride. "I have to remind myself on a daily basis to do the aesthetic thing, to look good," she said some years after her operation. "I know I'm not the body."

At Christmas 2005, Butch and she drove to Michelle's new house—Michelle had just married—but before she could even walk into the front door, Pam fell ill in the driveway. She was experiencing violent seizures by this time, frightening ones. In her last years, it was Butch who did the laundry, the cooking. "My whole job was taking care of her," he says simply. "I didn't mind. I liked taking care of her. I would have done anything for her, pushing her around in a wheelchair, whatever it took."

"I bet she hated all that," I tell Butch.

"I think she did," Butch acknowledges. "I think she wanted to check out to alleviate that. I really do. We had talked about it. She said on many occasions that it was time for her to go. And I would say, 'No, it's not.' Maybe I was being selfish. And she would say, 'It's time for me to move on.' She really wanted to see her uncle again; she was crazy about him."

"Do you think that your mother's death experience made life afterward forever difficult for her? That that's why she bowed out?" I ask Michelle.

"I don't know, I don't know," Michelle replies. She is looking particularly distressed, and I'm sorry now I asked the question. Then she rallies:

"I think it enhanced her spirituality," Michelle says. "Because if she was around anybody who was dying, she'd say, 'Don't fear death. Death is a beautiful thing. You're going to a beautiful place.'"

"Death is an illusion," Pam used to say. "Death is a really nasty, bad lie."

Michelle says, "That is one thing she put in big bold letters. That you shouldn't fear death." The first time Pam said that to her daughter Michelle was when the girl was 12.

On May 22, 2010, Pam Reynolds Lowery died, for the second and last time, at Emory Hospital in Atlanta. She was

53, and not sorry to go. She wanted very much, Butch tells me, to see her grandmother Rie once again.

"You will find this very strange," Dr. Greene tells me. "I was heartbroken when she passed, but I was also kind of comforted."

When I ask Dr. Greene what exactly he prayed for when he prayed for Pam, his reply is simple: "Peace," he says. "I used to pray she found peace."

I wonder, however, whether it might have been possible for Pam to find some peace while she was still alive. So many of those who have experienced death and then lived to analyze it and discuss it belong to monthly support groups. Didn't Pam ever seek out someone else, someone comforting, who might have had the same kind of experience she had? I ask Butch.

He furrows his brow. "No, I don't think so," he says slowly. Later though, Butch mentions a person I recognize by description. "One time, there was a gentleman—am I remembering this right?—with a motorcycle? He was in a motorcycle wreck? Or anyway, he likes motorcycles?" Butch seems to think that just maybe the two might have once met, his wife and this motorcycle owner who also died and then resumed life, an altered man.

And I think I know exactly whom Butch means—although the fact is that the gentleman he mentions never really did meet Pam Reynolds Lowery. He wishes he had, though, he tells me. Pam Reynolds Lowery very likely saw him only on the same British television program in which she appears.

His name is Anthony Cicoria. I have read that Cicoria gave a motorcycle to himself as a gift for his 50th birthday. It was not a good idea.

I have to find him and so many other people, the ones who experienced death and others who know something about it because they are physicians, researchers, nurses, scientists, and also family members of those who died and then, like Pam Reynolds Lowery, came back to life. Sometimes regretfully. Sometimes because they felt that being dead and yet fully conscious and aware while dead changed their lives, and changed them for the better. They were, if you will, enlightened by death. And the enlightenment never left them.

I think of Pam, despite her sorrows and her many burdens, as someone who falls in the latter category. She made a friend of death. Or it made a friend of her.

"Maybe my mother will help you," says Michelle, when I tell her about all the others I have to interview. She is very solemn. She means it.

Back in February 2013, when this interview took place in Atlanta, I was quite unlike Michelle, who says she occasionally gets signals from her mother, bolts of light that inexplicably travel across a darkened bedroom, a paper napkin that balloons and moves on a kitchen counter when there is no breeze (she sends me a video clip of that motile napkin). In fact, I was a staunch disbeliever in an afterlife, by which I simply mean the capacity for thought and experience after the brain flatlines. I was also deeply mistrustful of those who claim that the dead desire to communicate with us, the living. I figured that the dead were (1) exactly that, completely dead, blind, impassive foreigners stripped of language and desire, and (2) just perfect wherever it was they were.

Although I have to acknowledge that there were already certain notions and beliefs that were beginning to penetrate because of the mass of anecdotal evidence. Not every self-proclaimed death traveler could be an arrant liar or deeply unbalanced or both. There were just too many of them, and from what I'd read and heard, many of them weren't in the least peculiar—leaving aside their experiences, which definitely were odd. So by the time I spoke to Pam's relatives and then her doctor, I did already believe that we have completely misunderstood death, when it occurs and what we may expect when it comes— we have absolutely and for centuries misunderstood it, and we also have no accounting for why some people continue to think, hear, and see after death. When neuropsychiatrist Peter Fenwick told me, "With Pam Reynolds, we have a perfect monitor for what's going on . . . She got a lot of medication, anesthesia, they're monitoring her brain waves—so try to explain that!"—I couldn't, of course, explain that.

So perhaps that's why, impenetrable though I inwardly am at the time of this interview with Butch and Michelle on certain death issues, I somehow accept without hesitation or question Michelle's offering on behalf of her mother. I think, *Yes, this is quite an unexpected gift*. One way or another, Pam Reynolds Lowery, even though she is permanently dead and perfect where she is, will help me.

CHAPTER TWO

STRUCK BY
LIGHTNING

O F ALL HIS CONSIDERABLE ACCOMPLISHMENTS, Anthony Cicoria is especially proud of his chairmanship of a seminar for physicians on "Controversies in Lumbar Spine Surgery" and his published articles on surgical issues. He is a man of science, an orthopedic surgeon who is chief of medical staff and chief of orthopedics at a New York state hospital, and until he was struck dead by lightning, he believed he was on his way to a largely academic life, likely as a university department chairman.

I seek out Dr. Cicoria at a well-populated conference on near-death experiences, in part because he, unlike Pam Reynolds Lowery, is still alive: This is always a plus and not just for Cicoria, but for me; the living are always useful when you are trying to elicit information about unlikely experiences like recollections of death. Death experiences, it turns out, are anything but democratic: Only 4 to 15 percent of those polled in Western nations claim to have had them (the variation depends both on the nation and on the researcher), but even those percentages are problematic because a fair number of death travelers don't, for a variety of reasons, wish to discuss their memories with anyone. Dr. Cicoria does, however.

But I also seek him out because, both physically and emotionally, Tony Cicoria is the exact opposite of Pam Reynolds Lowery: a big bear of a man, hardwired these days to diurnal reality, incapable of accessing the interior thoughts of others, and someone who used to be—this was before he died—completely indifferent to music. Also, he is a physician who deals with the material, the touchable, the curable and incurable parts of us. Doctors, after all, are people who spend a fair amount of their professional lives fighting death: Death is the enemy. That's reassuring to me, a writer leery of la-la land. And at the moment, this moment, tape recorder in hand, I feel as though I am surrounded by la-la land.

By the time Tony and I have finished talking, it is perhaps 8:00 a.m. in Arizona, and some 300 members of IANDS, the International Association for Near-Death Studies, are milling about the hotel lobby where the convention of the once dead is being held. Here you can buy CDs of the speakers' talks or crystal jewelry with unusual properties or special oils and extracts that promise the purchaser tranquillity. You can attend chant circles, which particularly annoy me because I hate a lot of noise and I get scared in a crowd, but you can also hear some interesting anecdotes from the intelligent and resourceful, stories that sound unusual or surprising but not in the least fanciful. Many of the attendees wear large congratulatory signs that read "EXPERIENCER," and all about us, everyone hugs everyone else as people do at a reunion (which is what these annual conferences really are), although, as is always the case with any sort of convention, roiling beneath the atmosphere of amity, communality, trust, meditation, mass chantings, and the slapping of tambourines and drums, there are certain private feuds and whispered charges of possible charlatanism.

But Dr. Cicoria, although he mingles and mingles well, looks and acts nothing like the rest of the crowd. In fact, when we meet at the appointed hour for our interview (5:30 a.m., a time the surgeon particularly likes), my first thought is that Tony Cicoria looks kind of like a plump Sigmund Freud on vacation in Hawaii: a broad, bearded man with a comfortable stomach that protrudes inside a vast floral shirt. (On our second encounter, a year later, he wears yet another vast floral shirt—he must have a closetful of them.) He is a polite, quiet man of subdued erudition, and he wants, unlike many who greet him at the death convention, absolutely nothing.

It is, for instance, worthy of note that when I inform one of the organizers that I am writing a book on the subject of death memories (I am hoping, in vain as it turns out, for an admission discount because the price for attendance is hefty), she replies with considerable annoyance, "*Everyone* here is writing a book. Or wants to."

Whenever I see Dr. Cicoria at these conferences, he is always above the fray, a quiet observer. He doesn't hug; he doesn't feud or gossip. Long ago he acquired, in addition to his medical degree, a Ph.D. in physiology (his earlier areas of expertise were cell physiology and biophysics)—so if you had asked the old Tony what happens after death, he would have responded, "I really don't know."

A delicate but truthful reply, he tells me, "Because I had seen so many people die over the years. There are things that happen. They see things that a lot of times we call 'hallucinations.' And they're looking right through you and talking to somebody else. And it makes you think: *OK. What is it that we're not seeing?*"

And to a certain extent, young Tony kind of knew. He grew up in upstate New York, and as a teenager his sister Jaimie found him "sometimes callous and not always concerned with the people around him. He wrote poetry and it was often about feeling trapped."

In the old 18th-century house where he and Jaimie lived, both siblings say, there was a fairly permanent and mostly troublesome visitor.

"Yeah, there was a ghost, there really was," Cicoria says. "Everyone in the family had seen him, including my father, who was an unbeliever of anything. And my father woke up and this ghost would be at the foot of his bed."

Alternatively, adds the surgeon, the Cicoria family would be at dinner on occasion, "And you'd hear somebody brushing off his shoes and coming up the stairs, *STOMP, STOMP, STOMP.* You'd hear a door open and everyone at the table was waiting for someone to come in, only there was no one. And when I was little, my sister and I would hear these pictures up on the wall, and these pictures would sort of float up in the air and come back down, like what happens when someone walks by.

"So in my own mind, I wasn't convinced that when you die you just die," he concludes. "But I wasn't willing to go any further with that."

In August 1994, Dr. Cicoria, then 42, discovered another portion of what we're not seeing. He was at a family reunion right outside Albany, New York—actually a gathering of his wife's relatives, including his mother-in-law—the revelers clustering around a pretty enclave on a pretty day. All about them were barbecue grills, overheated children (Tony's three included) racing in and out of a pavilion packed with indoor activities, which you entered by climbing a lot of steps. In the midst of all this activity, the doctor set down his barbecue grilling fork and went to one of the outdoor pay phones attached to the pavilion in order to call his mother. He let her phone ring maybe eight times before deciding she wasn't at home, and anyway, it was the better part of wisdom to walk away from the instrument—really, really fast. In the distance, he heard a rumble of thunder, saw the sky darkening, and yet in certain parts, it had grown ominously illuminated. In fact, as he was about to hang up, he saw the very thing his mother had always warned him against: a flash of lightning leaping out of the phone.

It hit him smack in the face, a bright sharp bolt of purest agony and enormous force. It was like being kicked by a horse, it was that powerful. He was thrown backward. And then the oddest thing occurred. He didn't lose consciousness, not at all. But he did defy the laws of physics.

"Suddenly I found myself going forwards," he says. He was, he recalls, propelled by some force, unseen, although the rest of what occurred was perfectly visible. There, clear as day, was his mother-in-law: At the top of the pavilion steps when the lightning bolt first struck, she was now tearing down those same steps, Tony saw, begging for help. She was screaming, horrified, and completely deaf and blind to Tony's own signals.

Hello! He called out. *I'm here! I'm here!*

Deaf to his pleas, his mother-in-law ran right past him. Tony turned his head, and that's when he saw his body. It was lying on the ground, perfectly still.

Holy s—t! Cicoria said to himself. *I'm dead.*

But at the same time, he was also thinking with the dispassion so common to those who have experienced death: *Whoever is over there on the ground is a shell. So whoever I am now, I am. And always am.*

Nonetheless, there were things he felt he had to do while dead. Perhaps see his children for the last time? He tried mounting the pavilion stairs, but after four small steps, he found that his legs hurt. *This can't be good,* the doctor told himself, and just then, as he looked down at his body struggling to climb those steps, he realized he was starting to vanish. He was becoming, he recalls, "amorphous, no shape."

And then even that changed. He saw himself turning into a ball of light, round, bluish white, and he knew somehow it was pure energy.

It was this transformation into light, he adds, that allowed him as he reached the top of the stairs to travel through pavilion walls, his trajectory for some reason always diagonal. He moved diagonally through the room, silently, invisibly watching his children, who were having their faces painted.

I am never going to see them again, Tony told himself, watching the bright colors being applied to their chubby cheeks. But he felt no particular pang at the thought of being forever separated from his offspring. They had been his, and he had loved them and lived with them and his wife, Nina, but all of them were part of his past. When he was alive. Ambition, surgery, academics, chairmanships—

all that was gone. Besides, as he puts it, he was too busy floating diagonally out of the room, too occupied in marveling at what came next:

"That's when things really became interesting, and the pace picked up," he reflects. "Suddenly, I became immersed in this bluish white light—if you can imagine being in crystal clear water and having the sun shine through it, it was a lot like that," he says. But even more important, he felt a sense of what he calls "absolute love."

Dr. Cicoria realizes these days how overused and trite that phrase is—absolute love. "This sensation of pure love is something everyone describes," he concedes. "And nobody describes it well, because I don't think there are any words to describe it." But he saw it—literally, he insists. It was a force he could feel.

Being a doctor, he knew a bit about absolutes. "In science we talk about 'absolute zero,' which is the temperature where nothing can move," he says. In an odd way, the blue-white light was an absolute too, but the exact opposite of absolute zero. He felt it as an energy that could pass through everything and anything. *This is something I can measure,* the scientist in him thought, *it's that palpable.* He also knew that almost certainly the force, the strange blue light, was taking him someplace, and wherever that place was, he was happy to move with it.

What he didn't want was just as fierce. He didn't want to come back. He didn't want to return.

And with that thought, once again a decision was taken out of his hands. "Like somebody flipped a switch," says the doctor. "I remember screaming in my head, *Don't make me go back!*

"But I went back."

Looming over him, as he slowly regained consciousness, was a thin dark-haired nurse, possibly in her 30s, he speculates, maybe five-foot-four. She had been waiting in line for the pay phone while Tony was dialing his mother and lightning struck. Beside her was her 15-year-old daughter. Dr. Cicoria would never learn the nurse's name, or her daughter's. He wasn't in any position to ask, the pain was that searing. The lightning bolt that had sent him flying had struck him in the mouth, and the reason he didn't die permanently, he believes, is because the bolt lost some of its force, having perhaps passed first through the pavilion building and only afterward flared out of the phone, hitting him on the left side of his lips. It had then exited through his left foot.

As he returned to life, both those parts of his body were in agony. And his torso wasn't feeling that great either. The dark-haired nurse was applying cardiopulmonary resuscitation, and that made everything hurt even more.

A few words flew out of his mouth, addressed to his savior. He would later be horrified by what he had said. It was so pompous and arrogant. It also made no sense.

"It's OK. I'm a doctor."

"A minute ago," the nurse replied aridly, "you weren't."

He never did go to the hospital to have himself checked out. "I wasn't thinking all that clearly," he says these days. Besides, he knew emergency rooms only too well: "I'd have to sit there for four hours, and I didn't want to do it. Screw it! Take me home!"

A trip some days later to the neurologist. Another to the cardiologist. They both told Tony more or less the same thing: You seem *OK*. These sorts of situations, you're either alive or dead, and that's that. *You appear to be alive.*

And for a week after being struck by lightning, yes, that was that. He did ask Nina whether or not their young children, then four, five, and six, were actually having their faces painted in the pavilion room while he was dead—the same room through which he had somehow managed to soar diagonally after being struck by lightning. And Nina said, yes, the kids were in fact there, their cheeks painted.

All that was in its own way reassuring. He was now alive, all right, his death memories validated. And yet he was unalterably different.

For a while, he felt a bit fuzzy, "like a broken TV set," he likes to say, which was understandable. Two weeks later, the fuzziness having vanished, he found himself with what he calls an insatiable desire to hear piano music.

This was certainly new. The doctor was a child of the '60s, and if he liked any kind of music, it was hard rock, but of late not even that.

Now, however, all he wanted to do was to listen to Chopin. He'd bought a CD of Chopin's greatest works, conducted by Vladimir Ashkenazy, and was "smitten," as he puts it, with the brilliance of it all. From that moment on, everyone he knew had to listen to the Chopin piano works conducted by Ashkenazy: his friends, Nina, his medical colleagues.

And at the same time, he tells me, he was thinking obsessively about his extraordinary experience. *Why am I here? What am I supposed to do with myself now?* he kept asking himself. *Why did the lightning bolt likely hit the pavilion before it went through my body, thus weakening its impact? Why was a nurse—a nurse of all people!—standing in line behind me when I was struck, just waiting there, available to perform CPR any old time the heavyset guy in front of her happened to need it?*

The whole thing was all so orchestrated! So carefully and artfully crafted. Whatever that experience was, whatever it meant, it had to be taken, he felt, very, very seriously.

Nor was his brain, the pure analytical brain of a scientist, exactly the same. Not content with listening to Chopin, Tony had the overwhelming urge, after a few more weeks, to start playing it. On the piano.

Unfortunately, he didn't really know how to play the piano: He had stopped trying to as a child, after one miserable year of lessons. Just as unfortunately, he didn't happen to own a piano on which he might play.

And just as the doctor was dwelling on this sad state of affairs, he recalls, the Cicoria family babysitter happened to inform her clients that she was moving out of town. Would they be so kind as to shelter her piano for a year or so until she could make arrangements to have it moved?

So the doctor bought himself a how-to book, kind of the old version of "piano playing for idiots," and every morning he would wake up at 4 a.m. and thump obsessively on the instrument for two and a half hours, before going off to work. Every evening he would return home at 7, give the young kids their baths, read to them, put them to bed, and then pound on the piano until at least midnight, sometimes 1 a.m.

It was, he felt, a compulsion. He needed to play until he really couldn't see.

"Then I would stumble off to bed," he tells me. "And unfortunately, it really destroyed my marriage because I was never there. Any relationship takes two people. You can't have someone who's absent and doesn't provide any of the cement to the relationship."

Cement was practically nonexistent after the lightning had struck. Tony started taking piano lessons, serious ones this time, at 5 a.m., and he became pretty proficient. He wrote a fairly long composition (it's called "The Lightning Sonata"), which is packed, as you might expect, with dark bursts of chords and thunderous passages alternating with still others that are bright or soothing. One night he actually dreamed about performing this majestic piece in a large concert hall, with one of his selves calmly observing the other at the piano. A somnolent out-of-body experience, you might say.

But it wasn't only the music obsession, the midnight piano banging, and ceaseless Chopin that stole Nina Cicoria's husband away from her. Like Tony, she had been brought up Catholic, but she wasn't able to process the kind of experience her husband recalled. The bluish white light, the movement through walls, the glimpse of their three children, gleaming in bright paint—"That's not consistent with her faith, what she was brought up as," Tony explains. "We had many discussions about how can this be."

How could her husband have moved through walls? Been immersed in a bluish white light? These things seemed impossible.

"I think you're wrong!" Tony told his wife.

A decade after lightning had struck, the couple got a divorce. "I was shocked when they split up," Tony's sister Jaimie tells me. This, however, is not an unexpected outcome among those who return.

Over and over again, I hear stories of couples who split after such an event. And, I should add, many of those I've interviewed for this book have gone through divorce. The aftereffects are just too much to handle, for the traveler as well as for the spouse left at home, particularly since a fair number of such experiences involve a fierce desire by the participant never, ever to return to the relative tedium of what we call real life (and by extension never to return to the uncomprehending, totally clueless partner who shared that life).

The renowned Dutch cardiologist and author Pim van Lommel, who is a specialist in death experiences, in fact has devoted a major part of his career to examining them, did a long-term study of 82 death travelers, only to find, as he reports: "After 24 years, half of them had still not told their partners or their families about what happened."

Those who do confide, he adds, quickly realize their spouses often no longer recognize them: "This is not the same partner I married," van Lommel hears from his correspondents. And in fact, the partner *isn't* the same person, van Lommel likes to emphasize. "Their interests are no longer money or power or a big house. They have changed. They say, 'We couldn't discuss anymore what's important for *me*. I couldn't discuss my experience. I couldn't discuss my interest now in helping people.'" A pause. "A lot of hospital volunteers have had an NDE [near-death experience]. They know about death."

Even Butch Lowery, who had a steadfast and loyal relationship with Pam before as well as after the death experience she called The Knowing, very likely realized he couldn't possibly accept all that she believed on recovery, nor could he accept the notion, her stunned post-death realization (which she would pass on to her daughter Michelle), that "death is a really nasty, bad lie." Not then, and also not now.

"I think the kids want to feel her presence, especially Michelle: It kind of gives me the chills," Butch says these days. "I would think that as she's gone on, it's not as likely she's coming back to visit." He is remarried now to a cheerful woman named Carolyn, and undoubtedly the last thing he needs is the prospect of Pam's presence in the large Georgian house she once chose for him.

Butch shrugs, looking unhappy, defeated by the intensity of what surrounds him still. Then he says: "But maybe she is contacting them. You don't know what happens after life. That's something she and I would discuss sometimes. It's the soul's not wanting to leave. Like in the movie *Ghost*."

In the beginning, he adds, "I kind of felt maybe Pam was maybe not as ready to leave as she thought she was. Maybe she was still hanging around. I don't doubt that."

Adding to the general unhappiness of those who have left and come back, there is simply no comparison between the world seen, however briefly, after death, and the world to which the traveler must reluctantly return. Roaming through the thrilling realm of nonexistence, it turns out, is in its own way too much like an infidelity—and even worse, an infidelity that, long after it's over, is relived time and time again, and then almost always recounted to the very person who never took part in it, who never had her own share of absolute love and illumination. *I died and you didn't,* is the subliminal message. And also, almost invariably and even more infuriating: *I was a chosen death traveler, special and anointed, and for some reason, maybe a good reason, you were not.*

Small wonder that Dr. Cicoria couldn't stop thinking about the possible significance of his unearthly voyage. "I was desperately searching for—why? Why did this happen to me? What did it mean?" he tells me. And also: "What was I supposed to do differently in my life?

"And unfortunately the people around me didn't think like I did about the whole experience. Well, my wife, Nina, was—you know—why couldn't I get on with whatever's going on in life? But I was really stuck on, *I have to understand this!*"

And then the sudden passion for music burst into his brain, he adds. "And then I really swung out of control."

But the Cicorias were in their own way exceptional. Divorced though they were, they never really did separate. Not completely. Thanksgiving and other holiday dinners were always attended by both in the company of their children, and as the surgeon tells it, "It was always comical, because whoever you were dating also had to come for dinner on Thanksgiving." Eventually, Nina moved to an apartment specially built for her above Tony's garage. She was, after all, one of the few people who knew about his experience. Another was his sister Jaimie, who tells me she knew about her brother's after-death experience "almost right after it happened."

Jaimie and Nina were the exceptions, however. "I really didn't want to make it public knowledge," Tony explains. "Uh . . . ," he thinks a minute before responding when I ask him why he kept his experience inside for so long—more than a decade, in fact, before discussing it publicly.

"I didn't want anyone to think I was a nutcase," he says finally. "In my profession that's the kiss of death."

Another pause. "Perhaps I waited long enough for the consciousness of the population to change," he says finally.

However, at the same time that the doctor was struggling with a divorce caused in large measure by his experience, and simultaneously hiding that experience from most of his acquaintances, burying it really, he was also changing in ways that those who knew him found appealing. Gone was the occasionally callous guy who often felt trapped, says Dr. Cicoria's sister. "After his experience, he transformed completely, he had been touched," she continues. "He became increasingly sensitive to people, and very philosophical. It was like all of a sudden everything came to the forefront and he became a really good person, kind to the nth degree. He would give you the shirt off his back, he was that generous. He didn't know the value of money."

That was the appealing part. The more difficult part: Dr. Cicoria was, like Pam Reynolds Lowery but in a wholly different way, no longer easy in the same old world to which he had returned. Pain awaited them both, and not just the excruciating pain of a lightning bolt searing flesh or the pain of a skull that had felt the intrusion of hospital instruments. Pam Reynolds Lowery, suddenly and without wishing to, returned to this world knowing too much: the burdensome thoughts of strangers, the whereabouts of lost objects, the secret doings of others.

But Tony Cicoria felt the compulsive need to *do* too much; he simply wasn't capable of carrying on as he once did, single-mindedly pursuing medicine and academics along an unbending path. You might argue that since he pursued an extraordinarily ambitious series of simultaneous multiple goals after his resuscitation—music, practice, composing, child rearing, in addition to his busy medical practice—he was achieving as never before. When the urge to compose came upon him, for instance, any hiatus in his piano schedule entailed a kind of lyrical tantrum: The music itself, he likes to say, began behaving "like a spoiled child," demanding his instant attention and his return to the piano.

And he changed in other ways as well. Cicoria had always been something of a daredevil. Now, however, he was out of control. He was feeling—much like Pam Reynolds Lowery—that death, our current perception of death, was a really nasty lie, and like all lies, something that should be dismissed.

"He had no fear of anything after his experience," Jaimie explains.

"Like?" I prompt her.

"Like on his first day skiing, he would go down the expert slope."

That was the least of it. Shortly after his experience, the doctor and his family found themselves on vacation on Kiawah Island in South Carolina, famous for its golfing as well as the alligators that populate its streams. As he was walking across one of the bridges, one of his young daughters dropped her stuffed animal into the stream. Without a moment's hesitation, Tony waded into the stream to rescue the stuffed animal. Then he saw the alligators swimming toward him. Stuffed animal in hand, he screamed, "Oh my God! What do I do now?"

That's Tony, his sister says. In fact, she adds, a person could sum up Tony's whole life that way: "Oh my God. What do I do now?"

Not long after his divorce, the doctor tells me, he bought himself a motorcycle. It was a present to himself—a fairly disastrous one—for his 50th birthday. After gunning it up to 80 miles an hour on a dark highway, the doctor and his motorcycle landed in a ditch. A few years later, in 2011, he bought a farm and a tractor ("So I could return to the land," he remarks with some asperity), whereupon, despite his limited tractor-driving experience, he drove it alone and at a time when no one knew where he was. He landed in a pond, the tractor crushing his chest. It was only by sheer happenstance, what I think of as blind dumb luck, that he was able to summon help: His cell phone was in his pocket, reachable in the midst of disaster.

"But you know, with the motorcycle accident, that was pretty devastating; with the tractor accident, that was devastating," he says. "But it's not luck I survived."

"It's what?" I ask Cicoria. "It's fate?"

He doesn't answer. He simply says: "Everyone thinks I'm careless. I might be. My family tells me, 'You take too many risks because you're not afraid of what can happen since your near-death experience.'

"And I think they're right. I'm not afraid of death. I always pushed the envelope of life, but when I had my NDE, it allowed me to take it a step further. I take it to the edge."

"And what you experienced when struck by lightning," I pursue—"Was that a dream, a simple hallucination your brain constructed?"

"No," he replies shortly. "That much I'm sure of."

From time to time, the doctor thinks of Pam Reynolds Lowery, who—and Butch Lowery was mistaken about this—he never actually met, much to his regret. "I would have cherished that," he assures me. Nonetheless she is with Cicoria in her own way, and he has examined her remarkable experience. In public speeches, he cites Pam's encounter with The Knowing whenever he can. At times she seems to be the quiet figure behind these sorts of reunions: Many of those who have died and returned, among them Cicoria, are familiar with at least the outlines of her story. The doctor marvels from time to time at the bleak obstinacy and general pigheadedness of so many—the vast majority, really—of his fellow physicians and scientists who dismiss such experiences.

"So this raises the question: What is memory?" he says. "Where is memory? What happened when she died? She left her body. And there's hundreds of cases like that. But the neurobiologists—they're unwilling to make the leap of—*There might be something else!*

"If you have a brain that's flatlined, how do you remember anything?" he wonders. "I think it's pretty clear there's part of the brain that does interact with something we don't quite understand."

That final understanding—the understanding of death—will come, the surgeon believes (and he is not alone here) "within our lifetime." For the moment, the door is slightly ajar, and Cicoria, like so many others at the convention, has peered around it and seen something that isn't heaven, but almost. Almost heaven.

That makes these people one up on the rest of us. They have befriended death after experiencing it, acclimatized themselves to the future. Each comes away with his own particular version of The Knowing. They don't know everything about death, of course—Pam Reynolds Lowery didn't either, for that matter. But they know something, and that makes them quite special, distinctive—some might say, odd. But anyway, people apart.

Here's what they have discovered, and what the scientists, doctors, and nurses who stood behind them at the doorway of the hereafter have learned from their experiences.

CHAPTER THREE

WHAT ARE DEATH EXPERIENCES?

I MET DR. BRUCE GREYSON soon after I met (so to speak) Pam Reynolds Lowery. Dr. Greyson is a University of Virginia psychiatrist, but he is also something more rarefied and unusual: He is one of the first people many death travelers contact when they return. Death travels are his area of research, and he is responsible for carefully categorizing the sorts of travels, sensations, joys, frustrations, and encounters that constitute a true death experience.[1] He knows Pam's story, he knows Anthony Cicoria's, and he knows the stories of many others. In his files are more than a thousand similar reports—firsthand accounts from experiencers of every age: children, adolescents, young adults, all the way to people in their 90s.

After four decades in the field, Dr. Greyson is also what you might call a death travel pioneer—not the original one, but certainly the most important one working in the field today. He is a Galileo, having both suffered and triumphed for his science, and he is possibly the most prolific among his peers. His list of essential elements that compose death travels is broadly known as the Greyson Scale. It has been refined, reduced, and modified several times, and it is a serious attempt to measure and categorize the various sorts of elements that can occur after someone dies; the types of things an individual may, on recovery, remember.

These are the fundamental questions, pared down through much research from 90 to 16, that Dr. Greyson poses to respondents to determine the character of their death experience:

- Did time seem to speed up or slow down?
- Were your thoughts sped up?
- Did scenes from your past come back to you?
- Did you suddenly seem to understand everything?
- Did you have a feeling of peace or pleasantness?
- Did you have a feeling of joy?
- Did you feel a sense of harmony or unity with the universe?
- Did you see or feel surrounded by a brilliant light?
- Were your senses more vivid than usual?
- Did you seem to be aware of things going on elsewhere, as if by extrasensory perception?

- Did scenes from the future come to you?
- Did you feel separated from your body?
- Did you seem to enter some other, unearthly world?
- Did you seem to encounter a mystical being or presence, or hear an unidentifiable voice?
- Did you see deceased or religious spirits?
- Did you come to a border, or point of no return?

A fair number of the people featured in this book keep a copy of the Greyson Scale somewhere around the house, and for good reason: His questions, based on years of research, reflect the telltale signals of an authentic experience recollected by the once dead after their return to life. An affirmative answer to seven questions is necessary before an individual can be considered to have had a death experience, but the mean score among those the psychiatrist has studied is actually much higher, more like 15 affirmative answers.

Some of the questions on the Greyson Scale commonly evoke answers that to an outsider seem startling and completely unexpected. The first question, on time, is one example: Among the dead, time is not the predictable dimension with which we are familiar. In one of Dr. Greyson's studies, 74 percent of respondents felt that all incidents during their travels had happened at once or that time had stopped or had no meaning at all for them.

In the same study, about 20 percent of respondents claimed they could indeed see future scenes, but not necessarily events in their own lives, and 11 percent said they had discovered the future fate of the world. And perhaps behind this ability to see the future, there is another factor: a protectiveness the formerly dead develop toward their experiences and then project out toward the world they encounter. Around half of all respondents claimed that in the course of their death travels, they felt "united, as one" with the world. They possessed, in other words, a psychic intimacy with their environment that allowed them to know its future. Small wonder that thus gifted, many travelers resist returning to life—40 percent of Dr. Greyson's respondents claimed they were "sent back involuntarily."

Most remarkable of all: In death, untrammeled bliss is the order of the day. Of the 189 respondents who possessed memories of their travels, 74 percent reported "incredible peace or pleasantness," and 57 percent felt "incredible joy."

More than half also reported that, like Pam Reynolds Lowery and Anthony Cicoria, they had "clearly left the body and existed outside it."[2] This proportion varies with the sample and experiment procedure: An earlier but smaller Greyson study found that 75 percent of travelers reported they had left their bodies, experiencing the effortless flight known as an out-of-body experience (OBE).

As for a sudden burst of understanding everything—the fourth question on the Greyson Scale—more than half of the respondents reported a sense of complete comprehension, either about themselves or about the universe. Important scenes from their past came back to them in a process known among death travelers as a "life review." Their senses, many reported, were more vivid than usual, and they were aware somehow of events or odd details taking place elsewhere, as though they possessed extrasensory perception. In fact, the psychiatrist concluded some 15 years ago, the ability to know what is going on without seeing it occurs in 9 to 18 percent of those who touch death.

(A few other features are common to a death experience but not included in the Greyson Scale: sudden 360-degree vision, so that the top, bottom, and sides of things can all be seen simultaneously by the voyager; the ability to move simply by volition; and the capacity to communicate with those encountered during death without speaking.)

The greater the number of classic characteristics in an individual's experience, and the more profound each experience or sensation, the more likely that person has had what Dr. Greyson calls an NDE, or near-death experience. When I question him on his word choice—after all, most of those I've met and, I'm willing to bet, many of those Dr. Greyson has studied were not near death but were really and truly dead—Dr. Greyson smiles in his gentle way. Then he says simply, "That's the classic, traditional way of calling it, so that's why I use it."

It was in fact the psychiatrist and original pioneer Raymond Moody who coined the term "near-death experience" and paved the way for his friend and colleague Bruce Greyson. Dr. Moody is the author of the famous best seller optimistically titled *Life After Life,* a book that changed everything, including a lot of minds. It is a collection of the experiences of 150 people who had been pronounced clinically dead or had almost died. Its publication unleashed a flood of thousands upon thousands of similar recollections. Very quickly it became a kind of permission slip for the returning dead to come out of the closet and speak about death travels without being judged as lunatics. For the first time—in some cases decades after dying and coming back to life—any number of travelers were finally able to tell the world (and, more important, their spouses and children, their relatives and friends) that they too knew what it was like to be dead.

Dr. Greyson came to the University of Virginia back in the 1970s, and it was there and then that he met Dr. Moody, who had actually started his career as a philosopher. While *Life After Life* was selling hugely (three million copies and still selling today), Moody started getting letters from those who claimed to have experienced the very subject he had written about. Moody wondered aloud to his friend Greyson what he was going to do with all those letters.

"So I started reading them," Dr. Greyson recalls today. "Some were from people who had the experience decades ago, and they never told anyone about it! They felt they couldn't talk to anybody. So I took the box and started writing these people. I am still doing that now." He calls the experiences he has spent a lifetime examining profound psychological events with transcendental and mystical elements.

But his path—the same path chosen, for that matter, by a number of those scientists and physicians who choose to believe the returning dead, or at least to investigate their accounts—is often studded with professional pitfalls. Dr. Greyson knows of one surgeon who was ordered by his superiors not to discuss a famous death travel case with him; he also mentions two other researchers who were denied tenure because of their work on the returning dead.

"I was, too," Dr. Greyson adds mildly. "I have tenure here at the University of Virginia. UVA is OK with this because I publish in high-quality medical journals. But I didn't get it when I was at the University of Michigan. This is very common—because they're afraid their reputation will be one of nonscientific thinking."

And as I phone potential sources, I too get a pretty clear idea of the nature and intensity of this research blockage; this research threat, actually. Some physicians speak to me only after careful vetting; others, scientists and doctors

I know to have done serious work in the area, refuse to utter a word. Still others will speak only under condition of anonymity.

"They don't want me to talk about it—that's why the study of near-death experiences was stopped," says another scientific researcher who wishes to remain anonymous. He is referring to a certain group of his medical superiors. "They think it's not good publicity because it goes against mainstream theories. They just don't want to entertain the possibility that near-death experiences might exist.

"And at the same time that mainstream view is being increasingly challenged!" the scientist continues. "You see, there is too much evidence that just doesn't fit the traditional materialist view."

When I mention in passing this particular scientist's name and the nature of his thwarted work to Pim van Lommel, he smiles knowingly. It's pretty obvious he too has been on the receiving end of this kind of resistance. Which is why I ask him, "Did your colleagues drift away when you began researching consciousness after death?"

"Always," he replies. "But it doesn't matter to me. I was teaching at a top hospital, an 800-bed teaching hospital, Rijnstate Hospital, with a huge cardiology department— and some of my colleagues didn't want to know anything about death experiences. But when you never change your mind, you never learn anything! And most people—they are frightened of change."

Dr. van Lommel is an unrepentant Galileo, someone who can speak with exceptional candor on the matter because one of his more fascinating co-authored research studies, titled "Near-Death Experience in Survivors of Cardiac Arrest," was published in 2001 in *The Lancet*. All over the world, colleagues in the field were stunned by its publication. Until Dr. van Lommel's study was published (and for that matter, Dr. Greyson's, subsequently published in *The Lancet*), exalted medical publications rarely mentioned death travels—but that, apparently, is changing.

Although clearly it is not changing fast enough.

As a young cardiologist in the Netherlands, Pim van Lommel accepted the textbook definition of clinical death without question: "A period of unconsciousness caused by a lack of oxygen to the brain because either circulation or breathing or both have stopped."

So he was very surprised to learn, just a few years into his hospital work, of reports of 12 death experiences from among just 50 cardiac arrest survivors: The cardiologist had made it a point to ask each survivor, since very few patients in those days (and few still today) were willing to volunteer such information. Eventually Dr. van Lommel would conclude, through extrapolation, that over a 50-year period, more than 25 million people worldwide had such an experience to report.

Dr. van Lommel is now one of the foremost researchers in the field of death experiences, a physician who actually believed the remarkable accounts of death travels he heard from his patients and concluded that consciousness somehow continues after death. It is his belief that those who experience such remarkable events are able to tap into thoughts and consciousness that, to quote him, "are stored nonlocally." This consciousness is there, always and forever, hanging in the ether, in his opinion, without time, distance, or space.

If cardiac patients seem to be the preferred subjects for death researchers, and not just Dr. van Lommel, it's because they don't suffer multiple organ failure. Yet after cardiac arrest, blood ceases flowing to the brain. Electrical activity stops within seconds. Those who come back to life after cardiac arrest should in theory have no way of remembering what occurred while they were dead. Their recollections of death experiences cannot be written off as mere hallucinations, since—as virtually any doctor will tell you—no one can hallucinate without a functioning brain. Those with a lack of oxygen may become briefly delirious and then lapse into a coma, incapable of any cognitive memories at all. Low oxygen, in other words, does not—cannot—cause bliss. Low oxygen also cannot produce "lucid, well-structured thought processes, reason, memories, and sometimes detailed recall of their cardiac arrests,"[3] argues Stony Brook University's Dr. Sam Parnia.

Certainly low oxygen cannot explain what occurred to a 44-year-old man found comatose in a Dutch park, a key figure in Dr. van Lommel's famous study. The man was carried into an ambulance, where he received a heart massage and defibrillation—to absolutely no avail. On arrival at the hospital, the man was, Dr. van Lommel says, clinically dead: "blue—cold, no breathing, no gag reflexes, no blood pressure, no brain stem reflexes, his eyes didn't react to light."

In order to intubate this patient, a hospital nurse had to remove the man's dentures. Working fast, she stashed them in a surgical crash cart. After a 90-minute surgery, the patient was transferred to an intensive care unit, where he remained in a coma for a week. There was not much reason to believe he would survive.

Nonetheless, a week later he came to, cognizant and lucid (Dr. van Lommel calls this a "miracle"), in the presence of the very nurse who had first tried to resuscitate him. And he also knew that his dentures were missing.

"That nurse knows where my dentures are," the heart patient insisted. "Yes, you were there when I was brought into the hospital, and you took dentures out of my mouth and put them into that crash cart. It had all these bottles on it, and there was this sliding drawer which slid underneath, and you put my teeth there."

And sure enough, as Dr. van Lommel recalls, "The nurse found his dentures in the drawer of the crash cart."

Asked what else he knew to have occurred while he was clinically dead, the heart patient was very specific: He had exited his body and thereby witnessed exactly what doctors and nurses were doing to it, he said. From on high, he had watched the efforts made at resuscitating him and, he added, he was afraid that medical personnel might stop CPR too soon and thus prevent his return to life. "And it is true that we had been very negative about the patient's prognosis, due to his very poor medical condition when admitted," the nurse informed Dr. van Lommel. "The patient tells me he desperately and unsuccessfully tried to make it clear to us that he was still alive and we should continue CPR."[4]

Death today, in other words—or at least our ideas today of what death really is, what happens when it occurs, what is remembered after it occurs, what can be done and undone— is significantly different from the death of yesterday.

September 13, 2013. From a 4:30 a.m. phone call to a resident of Chevy Chase, Maryland: "Hi. I'm your brother's heart surgeon. I'm calling to update you on your brother's condition. Frankly, he had a very difficult night. He has crossed over the River Styx, and we are wheeling him into surgery right now to try to snatch him back."

This is the new paradigm, and it is happening all the time: The dead are being plucked from the River Styx—the great river in Greek mythology that represented a one-way passage to death—and brought back to life.

And yet to this day, even though many doctors know it is no longer accurate, if you look up the condition we call clinical death in any medical dictionary, you'll find the same sort of classical Stygian finality: Death is defined as the cessation of all vital functions of the body, including the heartbeat, brain activity (including brain stem), and breathing. It is a process, goes the prevailing theory, of successive and total abandonment: no response to pain or light, no breath, no thought, no sight, no speech, no hearing, no emotions, no memory, no nothing.

However, as more and more scientists are beginning to suspect, clinical death doesn't necessarily always and inevitably herald mind death. As the neuropsychiatrist Peter Fenwick puts it, "Dying isn't a mere switching off. It's much more complex than that."

"The key thing to understand is that many hours after death, it is all potentially reversible," says Dr. Parnia. "And that is why there's a need for more investment in research—because there's a window of opportunity to look at what's happening after death. There have been cases in history where people who went beyond the threshold of death could have been revived. So now when people die, we have a few hours—at least four hours, probably more, to resuscitate." And during those precious hours, he adds, we have "a window of opportunity to look at what forever had been thought of as an impossibility: what they saw when they died!"

So the age of Lazarus, as Dr. Parnia likes to call it, is upon us. The business of bringing back the dead has been rapidly improved within just decades: Cardiopulmonary resuscitation, which became widespread in the 1960s with chest compressions and mouth-to-mouth ventilation, was followed by defibrillation in the 1980s, and still further enhanced in this century with advanced body-cooling techniques that slow down cell decay.[5] Pam Reynolds Lowery was by no means the only person to receive the more advanced form of resuscitation. The body of Anthony Cicoria, pierced by lightning, benefited from the simpler version of resuscitation, deployed by a nurse who happened to be nearby. We raise the dead all the time. And the dead can return to the living, just as the living can pass on to death on either a temporary or permanent basis. A fair number of passengers along the River Styx can now be rowed back.

Can we go on thinking, experiencing, and recollecting experiences during that kind of temporary death? In a five-year study of patients who had undergone deep hypothermic cardiocirculatory arrest, Mario Beauregard, a neuroscience researcher at the University of Montreal, suggested the answer is yes, some of us—a few of us—absolutely can. Out of 33 patients with defective aortas who had to undergo cardiocirculatory arrest—their bodies cooled while the aortas were repaired—three reported after recovery what Dr. Beauregard refers to as "conscious mental activity." Even though all blood flow to their brain had ceased, they had lucid mental experiences.

So dead people are coming back to life regularly, in significant numbers, and, just as spectacularly, from 10 to 20 percent of the revived return with some memory of what occurred, or what they believe occurred, while they were dead.[6] That much is incontrovertible. In fact, in 1982, a Gallup poll discovered that some eight million American adults had such recollections.

However—and this is an important *however*—since death is not an instantaneous process, it is likely that something, bursts of electrical activity for example, may be going on while the process continues. And it is also possible for the death process to be halted. "If you think of death as a stroke, then you realize that, like a stroke, it can be reversed," Dr. Parnia tells me. In fact, he adds, if the *Titanic* sank today in a frigid ocean, with passengers gradually turning into blocks of ice, "we would have been able to save those passengers after they died."

But what exactly is happening to the human brain after that initial death stroke?

Here too some scientists are beginning to discover certain answers:

"The whole death process seems to be a loosening of consciousness," says Dr. Fenwick. "There is another reality then when the mind may work differently. This is at the moment of death. If the observations are correct, it's very difficult to fit it into our threshold. So maybe consciousness isn't brain-based at that moment of death. We need more data."

Moreover, Dr. Fenwick adds, "There is data that suggests there are faster frequencies in the brain after death, and that may suggest there's a residual consciousness of some sort. It occurs 10 to 15 minutes after what we would call brain stem death."

All around us, the boundaries between the two worlds, life and obliteration, existence and dissolution, brain function and brain death, are disintegrating, only remarkably few people seem to know about those collapsing perimeters. Or even if they do know, they don't recognize the consequences of what occurs when an individual returns with blissful recollections from the borderless realm.

"And now you have a paradox!" says Dr. Parnia. "Because you have people who have positive recollections for a period after death. And if mind and brain were the same thing, there should be nothing. There should be no sort of recollection after death."

If scientists are having a hard time figuring out what precisely occurs at death—and for that matter *how* death occurs—it's for good reason.

"The problem of determining what's going on when someone dies is that a lot of the techniques we have just don't work," says neuroscientist Andrew Newberg, who directs research at the Myrna Brind Center of Integrative

Medicine in Philadelphia. Our current level of instrumentation isn't good enough to measure many deep internal doings within the brain, and our modern medications are too good, especially sedatives. "You can have a flat line, but that doesn't mean there isn't activity going on in the brain. It just means it's not activity you can pick up with electrodes," Dr. Newberg adds.

This we do know, though: Some of that last-minute brain activity takes place when least expected. "People with what we think of as irreversible brain damage, like Alzheimer's, on very rare occasions, in their last hours, sometimes their last days, suddenly become lucid," says Dr. Greyson. "It is their own attending doctors sometimes who report this—and we have no explanation of how this could be."

I find this last revelation unusually compelling, because a good three years have passed since my mother's initial Alzheimer's diagnosis, and lucidity, perception, understanding, common sense—all that has pretty well evaporated. In fact, she is forgetting most everything: not simply keys or wallets or credit cards, but the names of my children, my husband. My name, too. Whole sentences, desires, and annoyances are drying up before escaping her lips. On occasion I can tell she has something to say, but the words simply refuse to issue.

Once I asked her if she was afraid of dying. To no surprise—she was once a refugee from Nazi Germany, so death had dogged her for years—she nodded emphatically.

She would, I knew, do absolutely anything to prevent it. She ate—hugely, enormously, as though food was the last barrier between her and death. I was visiting her three times a week, and with each visit, she became increasingly mute—silent and yet struggling not to be. It was as though some invisible demon had stolen her tongue.

There was so much I wanted to tell her in those last years. Among other things, that when death came, there would be nothing to fear. That it might be, in fact, as I was learning from a vast assortment of people—not simply those who had died, but those in whom the once dead confided—quite an interesting trip.

"I was 21 years old. I was in Vietnam as a nurse—this was in 1969," retired colonel Diane Corcoran tells me. "And a young man called me over in the middle of the night and you could just see him! He was so emotional, he had been shot, wounded, and I believe he had lost a limb, and he said, 'I want to tell you something, but I don't want you to laugh at me—and I'm not crazy.' At the time he was in a pre-op recovery room in the 24th Evacuation Hospital in Long Binh. And we had a lot of things to deal with there. We had dying people, triage, all kinds of things you thought you'd never see.

"And so he tells me about this NDE which he had when he was shot. And of course at the time I had never heard of it—a near-death experience. He said he felt his body come out of his physical body. It was floating around, and he said he could see what was going on. And then he felt he just zoomed out—and eventually he was told he had to come back to life. And the next thing he knew, he was in a bed in Long Binh.

"He mentioned seeing deceased relatives, and he kept saying, 'This is so wonderful, it's so loving, oh my God it's such a wonderful feeling!' And of course he doesn't know what to make of it.

"Neither do I. But I knew it was profound. I said, 'I believe you. I think this is really an exceptional experience.'

"And so that was the beginning," the army colonel tells me. "It was the beginning of my mission. I felt it was that important."[7]

A Galileo in military garb, Diane Corcoran spent 25 years as an army officer, and for most of that time she was an advocate for those who experienced death travels while on the operating table. Corcoran also lectured about what she still calls the "near-death experience." And she did this, despite knowing what her fellow officers thought of her. "The first ten years they all thought I was nuts," she says without embarrassment. "I talked to every professional nursing organization there was, I talked to AMSUS [the Association of Military Surgeons of the United States], to the Naval Medical Center in Virginia, to the Walter Reed hospital staff. I would say, 'This is what an NDE is, these are the aftereffects; it's really important that you health care providers know this and can recognize this. It's key.' "

Not even the military chaplains could accept some of the stories Corcoran heard during her career. "It was interesting—you would assume they could get this," she says today. "But frequently they were like 'What?' Oh my God, they didn't know about it. This was really early on, you have to remember. There were no TV programs on near-death experiences, no books. And I'm telling them they've got to pay attention."

But how does one accomplish this within the confines of a particularly rigid institution? A sergeant drove more than 400 miles to meet with Colonel Corcoran: He'd had a brain aneurysm, he told her, and the death experience during surgery was especially vivid. But what disturbed the sergeant most, what made him feel compelled to visit Corcoran so many miles away, were the aftereffects of his travels.

"Those were really difficult because he's a hard-core sergeant," Corcoran says. "He felt very connected suddenly to nature, and it would bring tears to his eyes if he saw a hummingbird or animals or any of that stuff. And you know his job was to discipline and work with young soldiers, and he's saying, 'I felt like I want to put my arm around those young soldiers and we'll all try to work this out.'" This is a frequent emotion among death travelers—the sense of joy, peace, and pleasure mentioned in the Greyson Scale. The returned emerge from their experiences convinced that love binds us all, our connection to the universe unites us, and all conflict resolution can be accomplished through harmony and understanding.

"Did it ever occur to you that that's not going to work very well in the military?" Corcoran asked the sergeant. "I think you might have to leave." It wasn't simply his personality change. Quite a number of travelers within the military are traumatized, Corcoran has observed, and not just by their injuries: Practically no one believes them. So they generally say nothing.

Corcoran has long thought that the ideal solution lies in a massive military survey of all veterans to figure out who might have had a death experience. "Well, you can't get to anybody! To go through the military system—" She shrugs. "We've talked to a couple of groups but haven't been able to connect with somebody who could make this decision."

So the question is not do these voyages occur, but rather how do we account for them?

For an answer, I consult Dr. Andrew Newberg, the Philadelphia neuroscientist. It's certainly possible to hypothesize that certain corporeal changes might provoke perceptual oddities, Dr. Newberg suggests—certain classic components of the death experience. "From a neuroscience perspective, these experiences relate to the brain shutting down and rebooting—much like a computer would," he says.

For instance, he posits, the brilliant light at the end of a tunnel might be caused by the loss of blood flow to the visual cortex, which is located in the occipital lobe at the back of the brain. Random firings from the brain are often perceived as light. And the sighting of dead relatives might be the consequence of that brain shutdown, when incoming sensory information is blocked. Even in such dire circumstances, the brain can recall certain memories and images, and a random face, one belonging perhaps to a physician or a visiting friend, might be interpreted as, say, the face of a much loved dead uncle.

But these explanations are all, as Dr. Newberg stresses, speculation. We really don't understand why so many of those who come back from the other side return with similar convictions: that death is nothing to fear, that love binds us all, that relatives long gone can be nonetheless encountered, that in death the future is knowable, and the universe occasionally seeable.

And it is true that the brain does have a way of lying even to the living. Put someone in a sensory-deprivation chamber, and they will from time to time see light. The electrical stimulation of the temporal and parietal lobes during epilepsy surgery sometimes induces flashes in the cortex, which allow a patient to remember the past, see light, hear music, and even very rarely experience an out-of-body sensation.[8] (Although Dr. Newberg isn't sure all of this can be interpreted by the science of today, especially the out-of-body travels recollected by many of those who return. "Another possibility is that your sense of self might *be* outside yourself," he says.)

Still, there are similarities between certain very traumatic experiences of the living and those classic indicators of the voyage reported by the returning dead. The sensation of overwhelming joy or even deep tranquillity can be, paradoxically, provoked by pure terror or a fear of impending death. In the mid-19th century, for example, the famous African explorer Dr. David Livingstone was attacked by a lion that, after sinking its teeth into the explorer's shoulder, shook him violently, leaving 11 toothmarks as permanent scars and the bone of Livingstone's left arm crunched to smithereens. Livingstone, who would never recover full use of that arm, wrote in his autobiography that at the moment of the lion's attack, all fear of death abruptly left him: "It caused a sort of dreaminess," he recalled. "It was like what patients partially under the influence of chloroform describe; they see the operation, but do not feel the knife."

Livingstone had a theory about his astonishingly serene response to the prospect of imminent extinction. He called it a "merciful provision of the Creator for lessening the pain of death."

So that fraught Livingstone moment when he faced terrible pain and annihilation raises the question: Is the death experience simply the brain's way of consoling itself for dying?

A 21st-century evolutionary argument doesn't hold much water here. After all, evolution is about thriving, succeeding in life. What advantage is there in having a pleasurable journey into death? Also, not all death experiences are pleasant. In fact, according to Dr. van Lommel, some 1 to 2 percent—and possibly more, since the voyagers themselves may be reluctant to discuss them—are downright unpleasant or even frightening. Science finds itself up against experiences that cannot be observed or measured.

As Sam Parnia realized early on, there is no good measure for testing the validity of many of the Greyson Scale perceptions of the dead: a brilliant light; the appearance of a beloved dead relative; the quality of bliss; or the nature of a heavenly state where time itself can speed up, slow down, or simply stand still. But what is possibly—just possibly—verifiable is the out-of-body experience. To that end, Dr. Parnia, in collaboration with Dr. Greyson, came up with a fairly ingenious multiple-hospital study conducted with cardiac patients both in the United States and in Britain.

In these experiments, a series of distinctive images are projected high in the surgery room, images that could only be seen from above. If a cardiac patient reported an OBE after surgery, he or she was asked to describe what they saw as they separated from their body. If the patient describes, as some do, a bird's-eye view of the room in which they died and further recalls, say, the image of a giraffe or a lawn mower that had been projected, it could confirm this aspect of the death experience.

Few medical professionals would agree with Dr. Parnia's hypothesis that an out-of-body experience can be proved experimentally. As I know only too well. One evening, when I broached the subject of funding death experience research with a top neurologist at the National Institutes of Health in the Washington, D.C., area, he looked at me oddly for a beat or two. We were at an NIH dinner party, and I could tell he was deliberating how quickly he might change seats.

"Funding for those near-death experiences?" he echoed, when he managed to recover. "Why? Do they cure anything?"

And, as it happens, the answer to that is: Well, yes, they might. Among other things, they might cure our universal fear of death. In fact, in many cases they already have.

CHAPTER FOUR

BLISS

As it turns out, it really doesn't matter how you die or what you die of. Bliss, understanding, a deep, focused tranquillity: These are the usual companions of the traveler.

"I was in college, at the University of Maryland, and there was this one guy—he insisted on being my boyfriend," Tika Juneja recalls. "Really, he was just my study partner, and I kept telling him, 'Why can't we be just friends?' I had a boyfriend.

"But this guy kept calling and calling me," she continues, "and I kept telling him, 'Stop calling!' I guess he was just your basic psycho."

One night the young man phoned yet again, and after receiving the same negative response from the woman he wanted, hung up. Tika went to bed in a house she shared with her close relatives, unconcerned, unaware as she lay sleeping that her study partner whom she had once considered a friend was at that moment walking over to the house where she was staying, then scrambling up the balcony.

On finding Tika in her bedroom, still asleep, he put his hands around her neck and strangled her.

"And that was when I saw the light—as I was being strangled, I saw the light," Tika tells me. "I felt very peaceful, and the light was kind of—I guess you could say it was *stirring* me to go back. All around that light was blackness, darkness, but as I focused on the light it just got brighter and brighter."

Maybe she should have been in bad pain—of course she should have been in agony, her neck was being crushed. But Tika recalls no pain at all. "You just don't feel the struggling part," she says. "It wasn't that bad."

Within the brilliant light, all she saw at first was her mother and younger sister. But then, much more curious, she recalls, "I saw the little boy for whom I used to babysit, and he kept saying, begging me over and over, 'Don't die, don't die, don't die.'"

That was when she had no doubt: She, Tika, was in heaven. Her life until that night, she explains, had been "jittery": so much going on, work, studies, her attachment to her steady boyfriend. Now there was none of that: "I was in a peaceful place and it was calm."

The next thing she heard were the sounds of distress: Her mother was weeping, her sister screaming. And this time, it really was her mother and her sister, in the flesh, both of them terrified and yelling as loud as they could. At that moment the tight grip of fingers around her neck loosened, but when Tika herself came to and tried to scream, no sound emerged: Her vocal chords had been seriously damaged. As for her hearing, it was so impaired that her doctor told her, incorrectly as it turned out, that the loss would be permanent.

When she was finally well enough to gaze into a mirror, she found a stranger staring back: the face she once knew now green and swollen, its eyes bulging and bloodshot from broken vessels.

Eventually, the wounds healed, her face regained its color. The assailant never reappeared (in fact, after the police came, he was kicked out of school and ordered to stay away from her). But for Tika, everything changed from that moment on, although perhaps not in a way you might expect.

"Before that experience, I had always been afraid of death," she tells me. "After that experience I wasn't. I knew it was peaceful, very peaceful. It was heaven."

I am beginning this chapter on bliss—or heaven as some here will describe it or at least interpret it—with strangulation because it is natural to assume that a vicious, unexpected assault produced by an enraged aggressor would also produce a terrifying death experience for the victim. This does not appear to be the case.

No matter what produced it, a death experience is generally devoid of violence, and its advent has nothing at all to do with the manner in which the death occurred. For example, in January 2006, *ABC News* journalist Bob Woodruff, then embedded in Iraq with the U.S. Fourth Infantry Division, suffered a concussive blast from a detonated improvised explosive device (IED) just 25 yards away from the tank in which he was riding. He and his cameraman (also severely injured) were some 12 miles north of Baghdad at the time the bomb went off, and as Bob's wife, Lee Woodruff, tells me, "A hole was blown in the side of Bob's neck—it was shattered—and he woke up on the floor of the tank."

He had heard the explosion. Woodruff saw, as he would later recall, "My body floating below me, a kind of whiteness." For some moments he was enveloped in a painless universe, even though, as the ABC newsman would later learn, he had suffered serious head injuries. Once Woodruff was brought to the U.S. Air Force hospital in Camp Anaconda, a portion of his skull was removed to reduce the brain damage from the swelling. For 36 days, he was kept in a medically induced coma.

Lee, who was by her husband's bedside during his recovery, learned from him some of what he experienced. There was, he told her, "a halo of light" after the IED exploded.

"It was so good, he didn't want to come back. But he felt he had to," she tells me. The Woodruffs, after all, have four children. Bob also had a challenging network career, covering news stories all over the world. When he came to, one of the first things he told his wife, she informs me, was that "the experience was sort of like being in heaven." It was practically the last time her husband would use that word: "heaven." He worries about the "hokey" connotations of the very private space in which he lingered, the manner in which he will be perceived by others, television viewers especially.

In any event, as a result of his head injuries, there isn't a lot the television journalist now recalls of what he experienced: Those hereafter hints pretty much vanished with his recovery. In fact, Woodruff's case might be a paradigm of why so many of the returning dead remember nothing at all, or very little, of their experiences. The brain may erase memory as a result of severe trauma. Or something did occur after the lights went out, maybe something spectacular, but the individual doesn't on return choose to recount it, for fear of being considered odd or even insane.

For his part, Bob Woodruff returned to the living, but— like so many of those I've either studied or spoken to—not without a certain amount of longing: "Hopefully," he writes when we correspond briefly, "someday I will live it again."

Which is the way most travelers feel. The way they got to the promised land is irrelevant. The point is, they generally feel, they got there. And it's waiting for their return.

"All I remember thinking is *WOW!!!* It's all so ordered and it's working," Bill Taylor tells me, reflecting not on his death travels but on his joyful perception of city life after he returned from those travels and gazed out his hospital window. There they were: the urban pedestrians obeying red and green lights, the neat, orderly lines of cars moving up the driveway. Watching all this clockwork motion made him, for some reason, absurdly happy. Beyond this jubilant acceptance of order in the universe, however, there wasn't a lot of reason for the patient's blissful state. Taylor had recently suffered three cardiac arrests in succession in a Baltimore hospital. These were followed by a seizure, and then two weeks in the intensive care unit. On recovery, all he could think over and over again was, "There's no chaos out there. It's amazing to be alive and to see this: the street, the traffic light, people walking. There is a process!"

There had been chaos inside Taylor's body, however, and plenty of it: a bundle branch block in his heart, which meant it could no longer effectively control electrical impulses. In fact, prior to admission at Johns Hopkins, the bottom portion of Taylor's heart hadn't been beating at all.

Some weeks later, he found himself talking to his wife: "Everything that's happening, it's all OK," he told her. At the time Taylor had absolutely no idea what he had meant by such an oblique remark. All he knew was: He meant it. Everything that happens in the world occurs for a reason, he now realized—nothing is haphazard: His death experience had taught him that much. This is not an uncommon conclusion among death voyagers who return. They have to adopt a philosophy in order to make sense not only of the experience but also of the reason they were allowed to glimpse death itself and then move forward. However, the nature of the voyage itself, Bill's voyage, was fairly exceptional—and yet similar in one respect to a famously recorded case that is discussed in the pages ahead.

Dead at 37, Bill Taylor glimpsed the universe.

Even his manner of entry into the universe was unusual: "For me it was more like a slide, like when you're a kid and holding on to a slide and sliding down and you don't know where you're going," he explains. He was scared, he remembers. All around him was darkness, and he was sliding into it much too fast, a weak, helpless body going—well, Bill had absolutely no idea where he was going. He was a computer analyst—logical and sure of his beliefs. If someone had asked him, "Do you believe in God?" he would have said, "Yes." He went to a Methodist church, infrequently. But that about summed up his religious or spiritual convictions. Taylor had always assumed that death was death: Nothing happened.

And yet when his heart gave out, there he was, he realized, at the bottom of a long fearful slide, a helpless descent into darkness. And then: "The next thing I knew, I was out in space, looking on all the stars and the planets," he recalls. "The universe was in front of me and nothing seemed to be behind me.

"And being out there, I could see everything was connected to everything else. There were threads connecting all of the bodies in the universe. And I am also connected to all these forms. Because I can see the threads connecting me to all of the stars and planets as well.

"These connecting threads weren't solid or physical, though," he continues.[1] "The threads were energy—and it was love that connected everything to everything."

Out in space, he felt neither cold nor heat, he recalls, only joy and what he calls "a perfect temperature." Thoughts came to him, relatively banal ones compared to the dazzling drama of his new surroundings: *So this is what it's all about! I'm still here and alive! I can still see! I can still think!* Ask Bill Taylor if from his death vantage point he saw Earth spinning on its axis, and he'll reply, "I don't know if I saw Earth. I didn't see the moon. You are farther back than that. To me, they were light, light objects. The stars were out there—just like we see with a telescope. It's like the whole universe is in front of you. It's just unique, and I don't know how to describe it."

The neuropsychiatrist Peter Fenwick knows something about this kind of experience, although, as he acknowledges, it is pretty rare. "A very small group of people go to a stage where their form dissolves into energy, they become—their words—part of universal energy, and they move towards a point which is in fact the grand state of the universe with which they will finally merge," he tells me.

"The whole thing is consciousness, and people talk about how they are refined by the experience," Dr. Fenwick continues. "You go through a period always of refinement. One of the things that happens as you die is the ego structures themselves go away."

"I realized that in that realm that I was—we are—just pure consciousness," says Anita Moorjani, who was born in India and was supposed to have died of end-stage lymphoma on February 2, 2006.[2] That's what her oncologists warned her family would happen after her four-year struggle with the illness ended with her slipping into a deep coma. But it was precisely during this 30-hour coma, Moorjani recalls, that she realized what last moments actually encompass: "We lose our egos, our beliefs, our gender, our race, our values—all of it goes with the body."

In that strange realm, time didn't run linearly, she adds. "Everything was happening at the same time." She felt, she says, as though she was in an envelope surrounded—just like Bill Taylor—by "pure unconditional love." Unknowingly, she echoes Taylor's exact words: "I felt connected to everyone and everything."

By happenstance, Bill Taylor's glimpse of the universe in its own way echoes the strong indelible account of a similar adventure—this one embarked on by the great psychiatrist Carl Jung, and recounted in his autobiography, which he began writing at 81. In February 1944, Jung, already celebrated and even revered as a pioneer in the field of analytic psychology, slipped and broke his fibula. Some days later he suffered a myocardial infarction—a heart attack—and it was at that moment, as he would recall with remarkable specificity (a specificity even more striking than Taylor's), that he was allowed a view of the radiant planet Earth, dipped in color.

"It seemed to me that I was high up in space. Far below I saw the globe of the earth, bathed in a gloriously blue light. I saw the deep blue sea and the continents. Far below my feet lay Ceylon and in the distance ahead of me the subcontinent of India." Only much later did he realize how high in space he would have had to have been in order to see all these stunning landmarks—"approximately a thousand miles!"

Jung just knew, he adds, "that I was on the point of departing from earth." He was delighted to be able to escape it.[3]

Like Taylor, Jung acknowledged some impediments to what was viewable from on high: "My field of vision did not include the whole earth, but its global shape was plainly distinguishable and its outlines shone with a silvery gleam through that wonderful blue light. In many places the globe seemed coloured, or spotted dark green like oxidised silver." Within these blues and greens, Jung managed to make out the Mediterranean, "the reddish yellow desert of Arabia" and "the snow-covered Himalayas." He saw what he described as a dark block of stone "about the size of my house, or even bigger," floating in space, as he was, and it reminded Jung of the tawny granite stones he had once seen along the coast of the Bay of Bengal. Inside there were flickering lights, the burning of coconut oil. Outside at the entrance was a Hindu worshipper dressed in white.

That mammoth block of stone was a temple, Jung realized, and if he entered it, the whole purpose of his life, the mystery of existence, would be explained. As he approached the steps leading to the entrance, he felt as though everything he had ever been or desired was somehow stripped away—and yet at the same time he felt as though he were a bundle of everything that had gone before. He never did manage to go inside that temple. The face of his own medical doctor appeared to him in this other world, forbidding entry. "The painful defoliation process had been in vain, and I was not allowed to enter the temple, to join the people in whose company I belonged," Jung wrote bitterly. "[I]t seemed to me as if behind the horizon of the cosmos, a three-dimensional world had been artificially built up, in which each person sat by himself in a little box. And now I should have to convince myself all over again that this was important! Life and the whole world struck me as a prison, and it bothered me beyond measure that I should again be finding all that quite in order."

The great psychoanalyst was condemned to life. For him there would be 17 more years of it.

By Bill Taylor's account, a thousand miles was easily traversed by a determined traveler. "It seems you could be as close to those planets and stars or as far from them as you wanted," he says. "But I didn't zoom in on the planets or anything, even though I think I had the ability to zoom in. Because any question that came up was answered. You had all knowledge."

"What questions came up?" I ask him.

"Where did all this come from? What's the origin?" Taylor replies. "What is this all about?" And just as fast as these questions popped up, they were somehow answered.

So this is how it works! It's all so simple! Taylor recalls telling himself by way of reply. *It's a lot of energy!* He actually said that aloud or at least felt that, he remembers. He believed he was being given access to what he calls "the ultimate of simplicity." What he was witnessing out there in space was an ocean of loving energy. It was quite unlike anything on Earth. Where he was, he realized, was heaven, "a place of no fear," as Bill describes it. "A place of intense love, of acceptance. And you know you're home, you just know you're home."

In fact, he was experiencing one of the central facets of what Dr. Bruce Greyson describes in his scale of classical NDE components: namely, the ability during death to summon an illuminated universe of complete comprehension.

So that was the easy part for Taylor, the sudden but deep understanding of who we are, why we are here, and where we eventually go—what Pam Reynolds Lowery called The Knowing. He felt he now had the answers to those metaphysical questions that puzzle everyone. "It was like taking the cover off of something you believe is very complicated," he tells me, "and then finding out there's just this rubber band inside that powers everything."

Taylor, like so many other death travelers, had to face a return to daily life, together with the visible doubts and amusement (or derision) of others, a sudden distance from old friends. Everything changes. Acquaintances, family relations, even belief in one's self and recollection of that extraordinary moment of metamorphosis—nothing returns to the way it was.

"You start doubting your own experience," Bill says. "You ask yourself, *What did I really see?*"

At first—while he was still in the hospital, in fact—he couldn't wait to tell his parents about the quite radical deductions that came to mind after his experience. *That you don't die when you die!* he kept thinking. *What great news this will be for them!* Only his family, he says, wasn't quite convinced.

"I said, 'What do you mean you don't need to hear about that? This is the most important thing I can tell you,'" he recalls. "But my family's reaction was, 'You were having a lot of medication. Or—it's just hallucinations.'

"And that's OK," he continues. "It's easier to talk to strangers."

His religious sentiments also underwent considerable alteration. It's not that Bill abandoned religion outright. It was, he discovered, that certain aspects of it had abandoned him or rather his new insights into the meaning of life and death had changed him.

"It was like looking at something in a whole different way. The smallest bug is just as important as what we call the highest animal, the human. Every element has its place. Every element is part of the process."

"And your old friends?" I wonder. "How did they react to the change in you?"

"My friends? They change. Some old friends don't want to hear about it. You just don't go there. But now I'm more open about it. But I don't impose it on friends."

Fortunately, he adds, there were others who had crossed over and received a similar understanding of life and purpose during their time abroad in a more remarkable universe—many became his friends. After some years of research, he discovered the most interesting of these: Jayne Smith.

Most people I've interviewed don't believe for a second that what they've experienced can be properly described as *near death*.

"That is absolutely true—I had a death experience, not a near-death experience," Jayne Smith tells me. A former actress who now lives in Delaware, she is speaking of an event that occurred in 1952 when she was 23, and in labor with her second child.[4] Those were the years, Jayne recalls, when hospitalized mothers-to-be were sometimes given an anesthetic called Trilene gas,[5] which they were permitted, Jayne tells me, to self-administer via a nose cone. The young mother-to-be was self-administering a lot—every time Jayne had a sharp contraction, she pressed that cone to her nostrils. Finally, after one especially agonizing contraction she inhaled deeply—in fact, she acknowledges, "as deeply as a human being could, all the way down to my toes."

That particular inhalation was her last. She was dead. Her heart had stopped. Jayne knows this because when she finally opened her eyes once again in her hospital bed, her doctor was standing over her. "And she was killing me—she was doing an external heart massage,[6] which I had never heard of, just taking her fist and banging the daylights out of my sternum. After they wheeled me back into my room, she said, 'Don't ever do anything like that to me again. You gave me a very bad time for a few seconds.'

"And she told my husband, 'Jayne's fine, the baby's fine. But I thought for a minute we had lost her.'" Much later, Jayne would ask her husband, "Did you ask the doctor what went wrong?" Her husband shook his head decisively: "Hell no! I didn't want to hear all that stuff. All I wanted to hear is that you were fine!"[7]

But that "very bad time" she had given the doctor during labor was packed with incident for the patient. Death for Jayne Smith was a gorgeous odyssey, unlike the accounts of death from anyone else I've interviewed. It was packed with drama, insights, understanding, and colors that singly and together formed a lush Technicolor screen.

Instead of falling into a few brief seconds of blessed unconsciousness and respite from pain, which was the intended effect of the gas, she found herself in total blackness, but absolutely sentient and aware.

This surprised her: "I knew I should be out of it but wasn't," she says. She wasn't frightened, but she was, she realized, confused. Somehow or other, she had gone abroad, swept into someplace foreign.

Then—as quickly as she absorbed her new surroundings—they suddenly shifted and she found the blackness give way to a gray mist.

"And I knew immediately I had died. And I was so overjoyed because suddenly I knew *We don't just die, and that's it*." Inside her large beautiful home, painted aqua and decorated with ocean motifs, Smith's eyes close briefly. "God, I can still feel it! I stood there in the gray mist, thinking *I just died and here I still am. And I know who I am: I am still me!*

"I didn't say anything. You know: It wasn't an audible outpouring. But I was pouring out emotions of thanksgiving and gratitude and joy."

The gray mist then turned into a white light, although it wasn't quite like the light Tika Juneja glimpsed while being strangled. It was overwhelmingly bright, yes, but Jayne felt that the particular light she saw was also "a carrier of total, absolute, unconditional love." She reached out and became, she says, "as one with the light." And for a little bit, she stayed there—"just lived in it," as she puts it.

It was a short-lived moment of stillness, however. The next thing she knew, she received what she calls "a block of information." She just knew, Jayne says, that she was somehow eternal. "That I had always existed," she says, "and that I always would exist. That nothing anywhere in the universe would harm me—ever. I could not fall into a crack in the universe and never be discovered again." There were no real words conveying this information, however, because she had, she insists, no thoughts of her own. Information was somehow or other being fed to her.

"I was like a radio receiver," she explains. "I wasn't having any thoughts on my own at all. Things were just coming to me."

Then within what she suspects were a few more seconds, she learned something new: "That everything going on in the world—there's a purpose for it all," she says. "That I didn't have to worry anymore about all the things we can't understand. The cruelty, the wars, all of that. I didn't have to worry because—I remember the sentence so well—*The world operates according to a perfect plan and the plan is working itself out in its perfection!*

"My own consciousness was so expanded by then that I was capable of understanding—everything. And knowing it was all true," Jayne says. "So for a while, I basked in this light, this love."

She had no body left, she realized: That had vanished earlier. And realizing all this and absorbing it—the dissolved flesh, the expanding consciousness—she experienced what she describes as her first real thought during death, and it was, she says, pretty devastating: *I wonder how much more of this I can stand before I shatter.*

It was precisely at this point of complete understanding that the bright light slowly began to diminish. Then the scene before her shifted yet again, and she found herself in the middle of a meadow. "I don't remember seeing the sun, but the brightness was beautiful," she says. "And the colors—oh, extraordinary! The sky was vivid blue. I looked all around and there were flowers, flowering bushes. I realized I was seeing colors I had never seen before—along with colors I had seen before: red, orange, purple, blue.[8]

"And I was so excited I could hardly stand it. So for a while I took all that in because I could see inside every bloom. There was an inner light inside every blossoming thing; it was coming from the plant itself. After I came back from my journey, I thought *I bet I was seeing the life force,* but at the time I wasn't thinking that. I was too blown away to edit much . . ."

The sighting of a lovely garden is culture specific, the neuropsychiatrist Peter Fenwick says, by which he means specific mainly to Anglo cultures, Britain especially. But observing within each bloom a special light, which Jayne calls "the life force," is not culture dependent: It is, as far as I can tell, unique to her experience.

"Then I looked up from all this," she continues, "and I saw there was a low hill in the distance, maybe a quarter of a mile away. And I immediately had the thought—*Oh, that's where I want to go.* I looked over there and saw this beautiful city where all the buildings were white, like white stucco. And I somehow knew it represented more than just a city.

"It was more a world. And I wondered: *Is that the world I've come from? Or the world I'm going to?*"

"I saw music," Charlotte Rohrer explains to a rapt death experience support group in Virginia. "When I tell people that, they say, 'Oh, you saw musical notes and you read the notes.' But it's not that.

"I *saw* music. You cannot talk about it to them! I keep ruminating over and over about it, and I just want it to stop!"

She cannot explain better than that what happened to her one summer night not long ago. She cannot explain the music she saw during death.

Charlotte is 40, a tall, blond, amateur ballet dancer and a former Intel system administrator who has spent most of her career, as she puts it, "trying to be Mary Tyler Moore," self-sufficient, industrious, "going where the money is—Arizona, New Mexico, Texas." Finally she came back home, to suburban Virginia just outside Washington, D.C. Her new goals: to finish college, enter graduate school, and become an elementary school teacher. It was all going well: Charlotte had at last ended a long romance that was going nowhere. She had plunged into academic life: physics, Russian literature, education.

But she had stopped taking her epilepsy medication since it gave her heartburn. It was, as she readily admits, a particularly foolish decision, especially for someone who had previously undergone seizures, of which she invariably remembered nothing at all.[9]

On the table before her at the support group meeting is a stack of books, intended to be sources of comfort. (One of them, which she takes home to borrow, is titled *The Complete Idiot's Guide to Near-Death Experiences*.) But it will take a lot more than a book with a silly title to accomplish this, as I can see straightaway.

Charlotte's eyes are red from weeping. Occasionally her shoulders shake with emotion. And yet her death experience, which is with her still—a vivid constant reminder of her failures and her triumphs, her fragility and her temporary reprieve—occurred some nine months earlier in July, when she was sitting on the porch of her father's house. It was late afternoon, maybe early evening.

She was, she recalls, under special stress that afternoon. A good friend had just died, and she'd been on the phone all day long, deeply miserable, mourning that loss. From the porch she could see the setting sun. She remembers that. It's the last thing she observed in life. Then she took a breath.

The next thing she knew, she was hearing a buzzing noise, and her vision altered significantly. "It went from compound vision [seeing out of both eyes] to this singular vision, but I did see a tiny mercury tube," says Charlotte. She believes it was then that her seizure started.

"Then all of a sudden I was just there—just there in total pitch black, a starless sky," Charlotte continues. "No one had ever existed. I didn't miss anyone because no one had ever been there."

The only living being she saw during this period, she tells me, was her dog, a Great Pyrenees named Otis. We are no longer in the support group, sitting on folding chairs. We are, in fact, sitting in my living room. It is a full week since the meeting, and still she is clearly panicked, on edge.

The inky black sky wasn't at all threatening, Charlotte felt at the time: To her surprise, she saw colors within the black. And there were other elements, equally intriguing and benign. "As a matter of fact, I heard what I thought was pounding rock music. Loud rock music," she recalls. "And I was feeling cool with a slight wind on my face, but it was also a little muggy."

Really, the whole thing felt like a ride in an amusement park, she thought—the hard rock thumping through the sweet humid breath of summer, the movement through a mysterious black tunnel.

Then Charlotte heard her own voice. It said, "I think I'm dying." She had the feeling she was dissipating, that somehow her form was dissolving, melting. "Going back," she says, "to the universe."

And yet—*This isn't so bad,* Charlotte told herself. The dissolution of her corporeal form didn't really disturb her. Why fight fate? Why protest in the dark? Also, as if to complement the tranquil acceptance that life was over, "In the black came this beautiful, beautiful cello music," she says. Thrilling music. The music she could actually see.

Then another voice sounded, a male's voice this time, unruffled, composed, and authoritative. It was coming, Charlotte realized, from behind her left shoulder, and it said with perfect clarity: "You made this. This is your reward. Enjoy it."

Charlotte had the feeling she understood perfectly what the voice meant. This then was her prize, the happy confluence of lovely cello music and muscular rock beating time to a cool ride through the amusement park of death. These were her last compensations for having led a good and decent life. And she had led a good life too, Charlotte felt. She was a moral person who had never set out to offend, hurt, or distress others. *This is how you go out,* she told herself in the blackness. *This is what you get.*

"I'm interested that the voice complimenting you on the way you lived your life was male," I tell her.

"I am too," Charlotte replies, nodding. "But I do not know who was saying this. That's one of my biggest questions too. I don't think it was Jesus. But who was it over my left shoulder? Who was there?"

In any event, Charlotte continues, for quite a while she was happy and contemplative in the dark—"Sitting in this reverie of amazing beauty" is how she phrases it. Then the male voice spoke again. This time his message was briefer.

"You're dead."

And it was at this point Charlotte felt what she calls "the tiniest little ripple" of dread as well as sorrow. There was, as before, acceptance of death's finality, but this time it was a hard acceptance for her, a lump in the throat. She knew the last message from the voice was true.

There was still more to come. The lovely cello music ceased. The calm masculine voice drifted off. But the experience continued.

And this is what Charlotte would be the first to acknowledge: That last leg of her death travels was nobody's idea of heaven.

CHAPTER FIVE

HELL
OR SOMETHING
LIKE IT

Although almost everyone who has the chance
to travel, however briefly, finds death a source of
abiding pleasure and contemplation for decades
thereafter, I have to stress the *almost*. There are the rare
voyagers who encounter either nothing but misery or the
kind of experience that is partly terrifying. I was really
lucky to find two of these, because experiencers who have
endured a frightening voyage usually feel a strong reluctance—an even greater reluctance than most travelers—to
recount their journeys to strangers. They are often the forgotten or the discounted, the pole opposites of Pam Reynolds Lowery, Anthony Cicoria, Jayne Smith, and even the
University of Virginia psychiatrist Bruce Greyson, who in

their own various ways constitute the elite, the ones who, as a result of either experiencing death or devoting their lives to studying it, have lost their fear of that final exit.

Either way—almost heaven or almost hell—the upshot of the two is the same. It's quite a ride. Eternity, as Pope Francis suggested recently, "will not be boring."

Charlotte Rohrer, initially surrounded by an eternity of bliss, would certainly agree with that. The summer evening that she experienced two seizures in succession, she found herself deep in the dark, the long quiet broken eventually by a voice.

It was, she realized, her own voice, and it seemed to surround her at first, then pull far back so that all she heard was her own name in an eerie stage whisper, as though it emerged from a ghost.

"Charlotte . . . Charlotte." It was as though someone else was speaking. But no one else was around.

"Absolutely me," she says.

"*G—DAMIT, CHARLOTTE! G—DAMIT!*" said the voice. Her voice again, she realized, only this time it was shouting.

It was telling her something important, she knew. "Look what you did with your life. All this petty stuff! You had this good life, but you did waste a lot of time being depressed and feeling sorry for yourself."

All that was true.

Suddenly the seemingly congratulatory words from the unseen male presence—*This is your reward. You made this.*

Enjoy it.—took on a whole new meaning, cynical, sinister, and dire. Charlotte Rohrer had, she realized, squandered a fair portion of what she had been given: There was nothing left to enjoy as she contemplated all the days she had spent feeling downhearted, drowning in self-pity. And not only that: There were other shortcomings, just as significant, that grated. "Yeah I've been a good person, but I have also done some bad things in my life," she kept thinking to herself. "I genuinely felt I was paying for the things I had done wrong."

Not big things, criminal acts and such, Charlotte hastens to add. "But for being shallow, for nasty, small crimes."

Her reward, promised to her by that unseen voice? The dark contemplation during death of her own profligacy, the spendthrift way in which she had tossed aside hand-fuls of potential joy in accomplishment. She had ignored or failed to pursue opportunities there for the taking. She had wanted to be a teacher. She wasn't a teacher. She had wanted a good, loving relationship. She didn't, at 40, have that either. Instead she had spent years with a man she didn't even love.

As the quiet male voice had assured her, she, Charlotte, had made all this. This was her reward. And "this" was empty.

"This part of me was really mad at myself," Charlotte says. "I f——ed up my life, I ruined my chances, the ones that I had," she decided. "My beautiful, beautiful life!"

A yellow brick fireplace and a yellow bookshelf drifted into her vision. She doesn't know why. There were no yellow fireplaces or yellow bookshelves in the house. Then from the depths of her frame, she says, she pushed and pushed—much as a woman giving birth might do—and awoke to her astonishment at night in her own bed. The last thing Charlotte had remembered from life, the usual life she was used to, was watching the sun set from the front porch. She had no recollection of going to bed.

She fell back to sleep.

In the morning, she got out of bed and, then, as the recollection of her death experience in the impenetrable dark hit her full force, she fell to the ground, incapable of doing much except repeating over and over: "Thank you God—thank you God—thank you God."

She was alive. She couldn't believe it. She had been dead. Now she wasn't. As simple as that. But not really.

"Charlotte called me at 9 a.m. that morning," her best friend, Lorrie Binns, tells me, "and she was crying so hard she was unintelligible. I said, 'Please, please, tell me what you're saying!' She said, 'I died last night! I died last night.' "

"She told me about the beautiful music and the voice telling her *This is your reward*. But then the last part of her experience occurred and she just knew—something was not right.

"I said, 'Wait a minute—what was going on?'

"Charlotte said, 'This is not a dream!'"

The problem was, Lorrie adds, practically no one around Charlotte really believed her when she recounted what had happened to her. "That was hurtful to her," she tells me.

∞

Listeners, relatives and friends, would tell Charlotte she had a psychotic episode, or it was a dream, or some vision she saw during an epileptic seizure and later recollected.[1]

Charlotte went to her local hospital emergency room, but the staff there had nothing to tell her except that what she saw and heard wasn't the result of a psychotic episode. She thumbed through the phone book, finally contacting—desperately—a neuropsychiatrist (her own neurologist was then on vacation), who patiently explained that when the brain dies, the abilities to question and reason also die, and Charlotte agrees that's just what happened. Her brain was dying. Everything that occurred to her that evening after the sun had set can be explained, she says, by science.

She had felt her form "dissipating away" the night before. "It was going back to the universe," she reflected. And she still feels that's what will happen when she dies a second time. "That's what happens to all matter and energy," she explains. "Our energy returns to the Earth and my body turns to dust."

That much she can accept, in a way. And yet Charlotte couldn't stop crying. She was terrified of dying. She now knew what it was like.

On returning from vacation, her neurologist told her she'd suffered from "a frontal lobe seizure." Charlotte is not so sure, however, that explains what happened to her.

So much remains unresolved. To this day, over a year after Charlotte's encounter with death, she simply cannot shake its effects, both the tranquillity and beauty of the early portion of the encounter, and the frightening second part, which was much shorter. It isn't just the total disbelief that originally greeted her account of what death was like that disturbs her— an account she usually keeps to herself these days, in any case. It's the dark. That still terrifies her: "It's too reminiscent of the black, the fear is gripping in my chest," Charlotte explains. Every night, she sleeps with lights on in the next room.

Also, the stories of death, anyone's death, now haunt her persistently: "The deaths of children," Lorrie tells me, "the deaths of those who die instantly—she keeps imagining all those deaths."

And, of course, her own death: Charlotte imagines that as well, "Because I know—that place again," she says. "There will be no coming back when I die of natural causes. It will be my time. And yet I love life!"

Her friend Lorrie thinks about that often. "I wonder if Charlotte is just scared of dying too soon," she says. "She hasn't yet gotten married, she doesn't have a child.

I think she needs to be fulfilled, to know she wasn't here on Earth for naught. I tell her, 'When all that happens you'll be more prepared.'"

Whenever an especially mean-spirited individual crosses their path, Charlotte will tell Lorrie, "That person is not going to have a good trip."

She feels in so many ways fortunate. Not simply because she came back from death but because she came back with a purpose: to do better this time around. "I feel it's extremely important for me to do the right thing," she says. "I now have a second chance to do it right. I think back on the times I was depressed, and I think to myself, '*F— off, Charlotte!*' "

Nonetheless, the way you live your life doesn't necessarily have a whole lot to do with the way you will live your death. And in this sense, those who return often find the teachings of their youth, the old, traditional Christian teachings, of dubious validity. The warnings of eternal damnation to those who stray or the promises of a blessed eternity to the dutiful and accommodating hold no water with those who have been there and back. All too often the Charlotte Rohrers of this world come back perplexed: They were good. They were decent. What the hell is going on in the afterlife?

It is a source of some annoyance to the less exuberant among the returned that certain death researchers all too often discount hellish experiences. These unhappy wanderings don't fit into the death traveler ideology: There is nothing to fear, death simply heralds the onset of light. Indeed, part of the reason for our ignorance of these more painful experiences is that for the longest time, if an individual's death voyage proved especially unsettling, it was either minimized, ignored, or discounted.

For example, almost three decades ago, when the death experience researcher Kenneth Ring commented on the subject, he noted that "In my own experience, having talked to or heard the accounts of many hundreds of NDErs, I have never personally encountered a full-blown predominantly negative NDE, though I have certainly found some NDEs to have moments of uncertainty, confusion, or transitory fear."[2] Around the same time, a U.S. Gallup poll confirmed that the number of hellish experiences was tiny: Those few respondents who reported them mentioned an encounter with perhaps forbidding faces, unrest, or, like Charlotte, an enduring terror at the prospect of death's finality.

And if the usual death traveler is reluctant to relate her encounter with bliss, love, and eternity for fear of being considered peculiar or unbalanced, the unusual voyager who has gazed into the abyss is even more disinclined to summon those memories. "A lot of people can't deal with it," Dr. Greyson explains. "They just shut it off—or try to."

Dr. Greyson, who studied 50 distressing death experiences, explains that even within such a relatively small sampling there is variety.[3] One of the grimmer sorts of miserable death experiences, he adds, reveals simply an empty, forbidding landscape—"eternal nothingness," as the psychiatrist calls it—which is exactly what a lot of us fear about death when we try to imagine what it will be like. The majority of such "nothingness" cases, the psychiatrist has noticed, "were reported to have occurred during childbirth under anesthesia."

Because she has specifically requested help and access to others who endured a similar kind of pain and similar bad death memories, when Charlotte arrives at my house, about the first thing I do is hand her the phone number of Nancy Evans Bush. As it happens, Nancy knows Bruce Greyson, and he has included her in his research. And as it also happens, she has experienced exactly what Dr. Greyson has described: eternal nothingness during childbirth.

"I went into the hospital, a perfectly healthy 28-year-old," Nancy Evans Bush tells me 50 years later over breakfast, before the International Association for Near-Death Studies annual meeting begins. "And then with me, it was just a—blip."

To this day, the former English teacher has no idea what exactly occurred while she was in labor with her second child: Five decades ago, hospitals were even more reluctant than they are today to inform a patient of a medical crisis; and back then too, as Bush is the first to acknowledge, she, like many women of her generation, found it unseemly, perhaps even a little pushy and aggressive, to ask doctors to explain what had gone wrong, much less to ask for her medical records.

All she knew after the blip is that a joyous event, the prospect of another child, had for some mysterious reason turned very bad. And then, after a time (she has no idea how much time) something else occurred—and it turned out to be worse than bad. It was crushing. In a way, she has never gotten over it.

Nancy Evans Bush is yet another of those rare people whose near-death experience was not crammed with gorgeously colored flowers, spiritual encounters, and unalloyed bliss. It took her 20 years to even mention it to anyone. She would never discuss it with her husband, not ever.[4] At one point she tried to broach the subject, but then it occurred to her that if you love someone, someone religious, as her husband was, "How can you tell him anything so horrible?" Of course it might have given her a certain solace to unburden herself. On the other hand, "Wanting solace is not sufficient if obtaining solace is going to be devastating to the person you're telling," she explains just an hour after we meet at the conference. "It would be exactly like saying, 'I had an affair.'"

And the worst of it, as she observes, is that she was brought up to be every bit as respectful of religion and what religion teaches as her husband. "I was a good Congregationalist girl! This all was too damn unfair," Bush says with mild amusement. The oldest of four daughters of a Congregationalist minister, she believed in Jesus and God both.

But more than that, as a girl, she had been part of the junior choir! She had gone to church camp! As a child, she used to sing, and with considerable relish, a Sunday school song called "Jesus Wants Me for a Sunbeam" ("To shine for him each day . . ."). And that's just how Nancy had lived her life, too. She had spent years, she insists, "trying to be a sunbeam for Jesus, with a sincere, deeply held love of what Jesus represents."

But when the blip came, Jesus and God were nowhere to be found, as far as Nancy was concerned. "They were someplace invisible and very far away.

"We were brought up in a period when it was really difficult for us," she continues over a hearty breakfast of eggs and fruit. "People pointing fingers, saying 'You can't behave like this, you're the daughter of a minister, you have to be perfect!' And I just wanted in the worst way to be normal—while . . ."—over the breakfast table she erupts in a throaty chuckle at her own expense—"while enjoying the special attention, of course."

So there was a duality to young Nancy. On the one hand, as Bush says, she always indulged in what she calls "quirky thinking." She wasn't really at heart completely conventional. On the other, she was also a traditionalist: She yearned for "the white picket fence" that would enclose some pretty garden fronting her Cape Cod house. That was her dream, growing up in Connecticut, and it's very much what she achieved. She married a fellow English teacher, a Congregationalist like herself. At the time of her medical crisis, she had a toddler at home. Things were going well until the bizarre blip in the hospital room. To this day, she has no idea what exactly was going on.

"I was either choking or my blood pressure had dropped precipitously," says Bush. "Nobody ever actually told me, 'Oh, we almost lost you.' But at some point I was aware that someone was slapping me, but I did not come out of the anesthesia. Still, I just knew there was something wrong."

The next thing that happened, Nancy continues, was this: She was flying.

"Initially this was an interesting experience, a fascinating experience," she says. "I was flying over a rooftop." It was the hospital's rooftop. Next, she saw from on high the windows of the classroom where she taught. And still she kept soaring higher—she had never been in a plane at that point in her life, but even so, Bush knew instantly that this was better than any plane ride since she could see every-thing in the dark: The old Hudson River town of Peekskill was particularly beautiful that night, the curvature of the river gleaming under masses of trees, bisecting dark hills.

She realized then that she was soaring even higher. Much higher.

"And then I saw the great beauty of this planet," she says, "and my immediate reaction was like a gasp. It felt like a gasp."

Oh, that's really interesting, she thought to herself. She was, she says, "captivated" by the spectacle. The universe she observed was a deep slate gray bundled in a dark night. And yet she could still see.

Another intriguing point: "It never felt like I had a body, but I was not wondering about that," she says. What preoc-cupied her for a bit as she continued to soar was this issue: Was she a mind? Or was she *in* her mind?

She had no answer. Not that it mattered much, because the next thing she knew, the absorbing part of her voy-age, her amazing new abilities—all that was over. She had stopped soaring, and was simply hanging, immobile, some-where within the slate gray universe. She calls this universe "The Void—a capital-V Void, because there was conceptu-ally nothing there."[5]

But within seconds, there was something, or rather some things, deeply unpleasant. A group of large circles, perhaps a half dozen, each one measuring, Nancy adds, maybe

18 inches across, was approaching her in midair on her left side. "They were black and white," she says, rotating her wrist to indicate that one side was white, the other side black, and that the large circles themselves flipped back and forth, so that first the young mother would see them as white, and then as entirely black. And although these big circles didn't exactly speak, they definitely communicated with her, she says, "telepathically."

This is the message they voicelessly sent: *You are not real. This is all a joke. You were allowed to believe you were real, but it was never true. This is all there is. This is all there ever will be.*

Immobile, lost in the universe, she felt a shaft of terror. Somehow or other, she managed to keep her wits about her, but it was rough, mainly because whatever she tried to communicate was somehow blunted by the voiceless objects hanging in the sky. They had it all wrong, she told the large circles. She, Nancy, about to give birth, did in fact exist. So did her toddler at home, her husband, her parents.

"And I was arguing with them telepathically," she recalls. "It seemed at the time to be brilliant, whatever I told them! In fact, I remember thinking, *Oh, if I could only have debated like this in college!*

"I was showing them proof—proof of my existence, proof of my reality, memories, facts, photographs of my mother and her family, and details of my mother's life. Now

I don't remember what exactly, but I remember presenting those details. I offered facts from history. I was just pulling them out of the trunk!"

But the black-and-white circles were obdurate: *None of that is true,* they argued. *None of that ever happened. You were allowed to believe that, that's all.*

In the blank universe, these silent communications caused Nancy to feel a profound and terrible grief. She believed absolutely the substance of those messages about her nonexistence, the nonexistence of everyone she loved. There was nothing to do but believe. "It was just inescapably true, and incontrovertibly true," she says. "Because my arguments had absolutely no traction."

It was at that point, Bush recounts, that the left-hand quadrant of the gray sky appeared somehow paler and lighter. "And I assumed that's where God was, because that's where the light was," she says. "It was like a late twilight horizon."

But this realization that God was at least somewhere in the horizon gave her no solace. Far from it. "God was pretty far away," she says with considerable bitterness. "And that was part of the grief." Because, she felt, if everything Nancy had been taught as a child about God was true, then surely God would know about her predicament, would come to her aid. Or at least somebody would come, she felt.

"Now why did I not call out?" she asks rhetorically. "Because I'm the oldest child of a Congregationalist minister who is not supposed to bother people on my own behalf!

"Now that's as true a statement as I can give you. So I'm sure Jesus has many other things on his mind. A busy schedule." Her voice is flat with suppressed rage.

"You're angry at God, perhaps," I tell her.

"Yeah. He, She, or It and I have had many words about this. Many arguments, many numbers of times."

The next thing she knew, says Bush, "I was back on Earth" in her hospital bed. And yet not really herself, and not really back. She had a new baby, a girl, true. She also had a girl toddler at home. She didn't think that her brutal encounter with the cruel circles in space was a sign she was damned or going to hell when she died yet again, because "Congregationalism does not have such doctrinal, lunging encounters." And besides, says Nancy, "I didn't care two hoots about theology because it did nothing but confuse me."

However, at the same time, she also knew that the grimly omniscient black-and-white circles were right: She, Nancy, didn't exist. Her children didn't exist, or her classroom or her students. It was all a big joke of nothingness. She had been told as much, and she believed what she had been told.

"It occurred to me years later that the grief I experienced was the grief of the suddenly and unexpectedly dead," she says simply. "I have never told anyone this before, but it's true. That it was as if I were killed and pulled out of my life." Not just removed from life, she insists. But violently torn: "I was yanked away."

So for years Nancy Evans Bush functioned on two levels: On one level, she continued her teaching, fed her babies, diapered them, brought them, as they grew older, to school. Eventually she would divorce her husband. Eventually too, after Raymond Moody's book on near-death experiences came out and then hit the best-seller list, she felt able to discuss her terrible voyage with others: among them her now grown children—two of whom found her narrative, she says, "vaguely embarrassing."

But even among those with whom she nominally had a great deal to share, her fellow travelers who also reported having had death experiences, Bush felt different, isolated, and apart. The other voyagers, after all, had been assured that the universe was ordered, structured. That it all made sense, and there was a reason for being, a sense of belonging that unites us all.

Nancy had been told she was nothing, and the universe she inhabited a figment as fragile and transparent as a bad lie. "And the fact that the universe was designing this as a joke was too cosmically unfair, unjust," she explains. "And that's what saved my sanity. That anger." The large black-and-white circles she had seen might be, she supposed, "authoritative," but they were, in the end, no match for her. She was the victor.

And yet, it is for her in its way humiliating that almost 100 percent of all death voyagers cherish the memory of their odysseys. At the IANDS conference where we first meet, the hotel ballroom and conference rooms are packed with those happy tourists, most speakers reflecting on their easy travels. Nothing about these death trips is hollow, vacant, inducing terror or doubt. Nancy speaks too: Her presentation is called "Hell in a Handbasket," one of its subtitles being "What Is Hell, Anyway?"

Although she has many friends in the gathering, she is nonetheless always the odd woman out. The cheerful voyagers are the vast majority of the returned. Those who return unhappy or perplexed or fearful are often ignored, brushed aside. It grates at her, being in the minority, especially considering the jubilation, the waves of relief that greet those who come back from the other side, ecstatic and assured. Those are the ones whose lives and deaths have a purpose, who return comforted by the knowledge of what to expect the next time they die.

"And so now people were saying, 'Oh, I've been there! And it's so beautiful! And it's so full of love and light,'" Nancy Evans Bush says. "And there comes a certain point when there's a silence, and it's as if the entire audience listening to all this stops breathing.

"And researchers weren't working on this issue, only three or four at the time," she continues. "And they weren't thinking, *Gosh, I wonder if anyone has ever had a terrible experience* . . . Why would they?"

She looks across the table. She has beautiful blue eyes, but they are infinitely sad.

So you are in a lonely place? she is asked.

"You could say that," she says drily.

"Have you made your peace with God?" I wonder.

"I am guardedly hopeful," is her cautious reply. "I have pretty unshakeable certainty that there is something we call God. Or what I call God."

Well then, I ask, "What is there to be guardedly hopeful about?"

"Guardedly hopeful that when I do die, it will be into the light and not into the closet."

I ask a final question of her: "Do you believe that there was a sense of overwhelming grief that was somehow transmitted to you by objects that were, like you, in space? Do you believe all this was real and existed outside your brain?"

"Yes," says Nancy. "I believe that."

❧

"OK—that, from my view, is not a near-death experience. That is a confusional experience," the British neuropsychiatrist Peter Fenwick declares decisively in his London office after I tell him about the strange voyage of Nancy Evans Bush.

"Now there are confusional experiences like that which are very scary," he continues. "I came into this when we were doing some experiments with insulin. One thing you can do is a blood sugar clamp."

He elaborates: "You can clamp blood sugar at a low level to explore what happens to the brain—just low enough to produce abnormal cerebral rhythms." One individual who volunteered for this sort of experiment, Dr. Fenwick continues, described on awakening, "a lonely, isolated, desolate planet, which he was walking across. He said it was simply awful.

"And I've come across a number of people who've had negative NDEs which are very similar to that."

In fact, Dr. Fenwick adds, childbirth itself and its effect on the brain may be the culprits behind such traumatic voyages.

On the other hand, he postulates, another condition often confused with a true death experience is "intensive care psychosis."

He has a classic example at his fingertips: "A patient reported she was in hell. She was burning inside and the devil was there with a pitchfork. And as she came to, she realized she was in the intensive care unit of a hospital."

The patient's feeling of burning in hell? It was the result of the warming pan underneath her, the neuropsychiatrist continues. The painful pitchfork? The needles with which she was injected. "That in fact is a paranoid psychosis," he sums up. "So I find negative NDEs—all the ones I've studied personally—fall into that category. Not in the category of real NDEs."

"Excuse me," I interrupt. "But this is you, Dr. Fenwick, making that diagnosis, deciding what is a real, solid death experience and what is either temporary psychosis or simply the result of extremely low blood sugar. To say that a true death experience is invariably joyous, to argue that if it's scary or traumatic, it's not a real experience but just a by-product of a drop in blood sugar, is a pretty arbitrary way of separating the real from the imaginary death voyage."

He has the grace to laugh. "I'm making the diagnosis," says Dr. Fenwick. "I'm using my science to make the diagnosis. But you're absolutely right. I like what you're saying!"

In his Virginia office, psychiatrist Bruce Greyson shakes his head when I tell him about Dr. Fenwick's line of demarcation, that bad death experiences don't count as classic death voyages. Blissful, illuminating ones do, in his opinion.

"How do you dismiss those without dismissing the positive death experience as well?" asks Dr. Greyson. "I don't think we have any grounds for saying those aren't as real as the positive death experiences."

He knows only too well what Nancy Evans Bush and others like her have been through. "Nancy has really struggled with it," he reflects. "And yet—a lot of them would say, 'I am so glad that I had it! That it happened to me!' Although it was terrifying when it happened and really interfered with their lives, they ended up benefiting from it." The bad death travels, he suggests, are every bit as transformational, even inspirational as the blissful ones.

I think of his words as Charlotte Rohrer clutches her knees in my living room. "So now I feel—I feel so grateful for this life that I want to create more joy for someone else as much as I can," she tells me. "It's an absolute gift. I wouldn't change it for anything. I woke up with this hyper-real sense—thanking God for life. I've been on cloud nine so long, with so much gratitude to be here!! If I have a stressful job, who cares? I'm alive!"

"These experiences are so powerful," Nancy Evans Bush tells me at the end of our conversation. She is 78 now, but none of what she went through five decades ago has left her. When next I see her, it is at my house: She will stay there for three days during yet another IANDS conference. And she will say exactly what Greyson predicts: Despite the injustice, the fear, and disorientation her experience provoked, she wouldn't have her experience excised from her life for anything. "When you wake up, you know that the world is more than you ever thought," says Nancy.

CHAPTER SIX

THOSE WE MEET

WHAT JAYNE SMITH SAW as she lay quite dead after taking in a deep whiff of Trilene anesthesia on her hospital bed was not simply flowers of unusual colors, their brilliance unlike anything she had ever seen, but also a low hill perhaps a quarter mile into the distance. *Oh, that's where I want to go,* she thought to herself, because there were around 20 people on that hill, wearing beautiful robes, like togas, but again in colors she had never before seen while still alive. They were talking to each other; in fact, the whole scene reminded her of people at a railroad station, just waiting. She knew she was dead, all right. Those colors, those people, those togas—they were nothing she had seen before.

In the distance, she observed, there was a woman sitting on the ground, just staring off, at what precisely Jayne couldn't tell. Behind this woman and her friends was the beautiful city, its buildings chalk white.

She wanted to talk to these people in togas, and as with most death travelers, her wish was granted without exertion, without even a single step in the direction of those she wished to contact. Desire and attainment of desire are all one in death, and the next thing she knew, she was there on the hill, and three men were approaching her, two of them with dark hair, the tallest—the leader, in fact—quite bald except for the white fringe that encircled his scalp. He was the one who did all the communicating: In death, according to those who have been there, there is no speech, but there are interconnecting thoughts, predictions, flashbacks, questions, and occasionally answers. Jayne got a number of these.

"The man who did all the communicating with me was the tallest of the three," she recalls. Jayne found everything about this figure "perfect." It never occurred to her to wonder if he was God or Jesus or Saint Peter: He had a long face, his features beautifully aligned, his manner wise and authoritative, and she just sensed he was some kind of spiritual authority.

"Anything he said, I could believe," is how she puts it.

I know what happened to me, I know I have died, Jayne communicated.

The tall man nodded: *That is right, yes. But you won't be staying here. It's not time for you to be here yet.*

What was interesting, she stresses these days, is she didn't stand there on the hill actually transmitting every syllable or sentence in order to receive an answer from the tall man. All Jayne needed, she explains, was "to have the impulse to say whatever I wanted to say, however many sentences there might be." Then that impulse would somehow travel to the tall man in the toga.

This form of speechless communication is very common among death travelers—it is in fact a thread more common than, say, entering a tunnel or seeing a light or floating above one's own body. As the Dutch cardiologist Pim van Lommel explains, his findings indicate that "[a] third receive information, but not by the body . . . They don't hear, but they know the thoughts of people."

This silent communication worked both ways, says Jayne: If the tall man in the toga needed to transmit an answer to her questions, "the impulse came back to me and I immediately knew what he meant to convey."

Everything since I came over to this side—everything— has been beautiful with perfect love. But what about all my sins?

The tall man responded: *There are no sins, not the way you think of them on Earth. The only thing that matters here is what you think. What is in your heart?*

Jayne looked into her heart. She cannot explain to this day how she quite managed this feat, but she says that's exactly what happened. She gazed straight into it. And it amazes her now when she speaks about it because, as she explains, her voice tinged with irony, "I was an

Episcopalian, and it's a very nice religion, but we don't get into things like that." But there she was, a dead Episcopalian high on a hill in Wonderland, "enabled to look into the core of me."

Inside that heart she was, as she saw on inspection, "perfect love. Perfection." Later she would figure out that's what everyone is: perfect, endowed with love. That this is what the Bible meant when it said we are all created in God's image, she decided. She had never understood that passage before. But all that extrapolation came later.

Standing in the presence of the men in togas, another thought came to her: "I suddenly knew how God sees the world. I understand. We have this core of God-ness, and it can get covered over by brutal experiences. But everything is beautiful, and I love it all."

Of course, of course. I used to know that—how did I ever forget something as important as that? Since I'm not going to be able to stay, I want to take all of this back. Can you tell me what everything is about? The meaning of the world? The universe? Us?

And the tall man with the beautiful features gave her all the answers in just a few sentences, Jayne says, adding only: *You can take back to others everything that's happened except the answers to your last questions. You aren't going to be able to remember those answers.*

That's when everything went black. Jayne heard a click, exactly as though a tape recorder had switched off.

"If I'd been allowed to stay, I would have asked a hundred questions," she says. "But it was over."

When she opened her eyes, she was once again in her hospital bed, her doctor was pounding hard on her chest, and it hurt so badly that Jayne somehow managed a weak protest: "I don't mean to be rude, but would you please stop that?"

That was when the doctor shot her a smile of relief and stopped performing the external heart massage.

Back among the living and unsure of what, if anything, to say to anyone about what had just happened, Jayne contemplated in silence her death experience. "I lived for 23 years without knowing that anyone but me had had this experience," she says. "And believe me, there were very few people I talked to about this. Maybe six people, and I never went through the whole experience except with my husband. I felt it was too much to ask of people."

Over and over again, she relived her death, thinking *I wouldn't trade this experience for a billion dollars. But what am I supposed to do with it? How am I supposed to use it? I don't have a clue. I can't even tell people and have them think I've flipped my lid! And I'll tell you this much: I have way too much respect and love for the whole happening to just throw it out there and have people kick the daylights out of it.*

Something else occurred to her: her complete passivity—surrender, if you will—at the end of her experience when she found herself exiled from paradise without issuing a word of protest. It never occurred to Jayne to fight the inevitable, to remain among the wise figures she had just met and perhaps live in the gorgeous white stucco city beyond.

Hers was an unusually limp response: Most of the once blissful dead wish to remain exactly as they were. Carl Jung himself recalled: "I felt violent resistance toward my doctor because he had brought me back to life."[1] And with ample reason, he felt. Gone, thanks to this doctor, was the gorgeous, mysterious universe to which Jung had been so briefly admitted, the one he had just barely been permitted to explore before being dragged back to the dungeon of an uncherished previous existence.

It was only when he woke up from a sound evening sleep in the early weeks after his heart attack that he managed to return—for a few hours—to the brief enchantment he had known. "This is eternal bliss," he thought to himself on these occasions. Sometimes he awoke in a paradise strikingly similar to the one Jayne Smith experienced: "a wide valley" at the end of which "a gentle chain of hills began." That valley ended in a vast amphitheater, Jung wrote, and on its stage classical Greek dancers appeared, along with the Greek gods Hera and Zeus, who performed a ritualistic wedding ceremony.

But the next morning, the drabness would always return. "What idiocy, what hideous nonsense!" Jung would tell himself. When the visions evaporated after a few weeks, he was tormented by their loss.

But Jayne felt no such antipathy or revulsion to her return to life. She had been told it was not her time by the toga-clad figure, and there was simply no use quarreling with someone that authoritative.

And besides, she now had a new baby.

Jayne Smith's death encounter, although not rare among those who return from their travels, is also not usual. In Peter Fenwick's British study, just 17 percent of the 350 cases he examined reported seeing spiritual beings after death— although it's worth noting that it is the mystical encounters with strangers that tend to yield the most insight (along with a great deal of frustration) into metaphysical issues, that they, in fact, seem to be a lot more detailed and enlightening than death meetings with, say, relatives or spouses.

The experience of the psychoanalyst Jung during his heart attack is a prime example of this more compelling and evocative kind of encounter. On the side of the unforgettable "gigantic dark block" of floating stone that Jung had glimpsed while dead was an entrance, he would later write. "To the right of the entrance, a black Hindu sat silently in lotus posture upon a stone bench. He wore a white gown and I knew that he expected me . . .

"As I approached the steps leading up to the entrance into the rock, a strange thing happened: I had the feeling that everything was being sloughed away; everything I aimed at or wished for or thought, the whole phantasmagoria of earthly existence, fell away or was stripped from me—an extremely painful process."[2]

Like Jayne Smith when she approached the wise men in togas, Jung felt there was much more he could learn as he drew near the stone temple. "I had the certainty I was about to enter an illuminated room and would meet there all those people to whom I belong in reality." It was those exceptional people, Jung was sure, who might answer the hard questions about existence and nonexistence. What had existed before him, Jung wanted to know? Why had he come into being? Where was his life flowing? He had always wondered about these issues; he wrote, "My life seemed to have been snipped out of a long chain of events and many questions had remained unanswered."

And unanswered they would remain. It was at that very moment, Jung writes, that the face of his doctor appeared "from the direction of Europe," and all of what he had come to cherish—the stone temple, the man in the lotus position, the unentered illuminated room containing, he was certain, "those people to whom I belong"—dissolved. The likeness of his doctor was framed by a gold laurel wreath or a gold chain, and between the two men a silent exchange seemed to take place. "I had no right to leave Earth and must return," Jung realized at once. It would be weeks before he could reconcile himself to living.

Dr. Parnia believes death is a process. "You see, there are two stages," he explains. "Stage one is when someone dies. And the next stage is what happens biologically. The cells in your body don't die immediately after you die. They don't work, but they also don't suddenly become annihilated. Everything has a process. Brain cells can stay alive for up to eight hours. The brain has its own supply of energy. So even if my brain is deprived of oxygen, it doesn't die immediately."

For his part, Dr. Fenwick looks at the death process somewhat differently. When death nears, he says, the lighting isn't abruptly extinguished, leaving the audience in the dark. "There's a new science coming out now on what is called after-death pulses," Fenwick says. "And what this means is yes, there are surges in brain activity after death. And what the data show is: If you have a monitor on people's brains after the heart stops, there may be a period when, yes, they are essentially dead. But the monitor shows there are huge amounts of brain activity again. And then the whole thing finally shuts down."

In other words, the spiritual guides both Jayne Smith and Carl Jung encountered very probably appeared somewhere along the road of death, well past life, but before the final turnoff.

The first phase, Dr. Fenwick says, is likely to include a premonition of death shortly before the event takes place. It is only during the second phase that a deceased family member might appear, often with the suggestion from this relative that he or she will be back shortly to visit the dying individual in anticipation of a long journey. In the final scene, while the heart is completely stopped and the brain flatlined, as Pam Reynolds Lowery discovered, a deceased relative might appear with more to recount—in other words, during death itself.

And in fact, when I interview Carol Gonzales, a nurse working at the Washington Home and Community Hospice with over 15 years of hospice experience, she tells me about just such a patient with a Phase 2 encounter: a man in his 70s, dying, as he and his family had just discovered after a medical exam, of lung cancer.

"It came as a complete shock to his family, especially his daughter with whom he lived," says Gonzales. "He had been getting weaker, but they were blown away by the diagnosis."

The adult daughter especially was devastated. Just a few years earlier, her mother had died of a stroke with no warning, and the daughter was still taking antidepressants and going to therapy to recover from her grief and shock. Now this . . .

"And most of the time, no one sits down and explains what's going on with a patient other than a hospice nurse," Gonzales says. "So the daughter and I—we get to have the talk. We talk about how quickly her father is declining and how he may not be around long. He wasn't eating or drinking much; he was bedbound. What happens to cancer patients, a lot of times, is they do really well until a week or so before they die, and then they usually take to their bed: They're getting ready to pass. So I started preparing the daughter for this."

After that talk, Gonzales returned for a visit. A week had gone by.

"The most amazing thing has been happening at night," the daughter told the nurse. "My father has been speaking to members of our family who died." This had been going on for at least three nights running, during which she had actually observed her father communicating, the daughter added, and he was not only speaking to those dead relatives, but he was also apparently seeing them. In fact, she recognized the names of the deceased, although some she had known only as a child.

And it seemed to her, she added, that what her father was involved in was not a conversation that was one-sided. It was two-sided.

Then the nighttime conversations ended. The father lapsed into a pre-death sleep, and finally died.

"But the moral of the story is this," says Gonzales. "His daughter felt that her father's short period of talking to dead family members was a gift. As a result of hearing this, she did very well after her father's death. She was very accepting of it. She said it had helped with her mother's death because to her, it was confirmation her mother wasn't dead, because he had been speaking to her too. And that even though her dad was leaving her, he wasn't going to disappear forever."

Often after a hard death, there's a follow-up by nurses and social workers with anguished family members. Not this time, however. "There didn't seem to be a need for a bereavement follow-up six months down the line," says Gonzales. "Her observing her father talk with the dead was a big, big deal."

On yet another occasion, Gonzales admitted a Florida nursing home patient with esophageal cancer. "She looked to me like a person who was dying. She was emaciated, bedbound, her mouth open," the hospice nurse explains. "However, she had no intention of leaving. She started talking, even with the hole in her throat—you can put something over your trachea to talk sometimes.

"And she told me *they* were coming for her," the nurse continues. "*They*. And we're sitting in her room, and she's pointing to the curtain over the window. She said, 'I told *them* I wasn't coming. I wasn't yet ready.'"

One beautiful day, the old woman's family got together, maybe 20 of them, Gonzales recalls, grandchildren included, all of them picnicking on the patio of the nursing home. The old woman was pleased, says Gonzales, ready for her next step. Some 11 days later, her patient died, very peacefully, says the nurse: Whatever group was coming for her waited until she had met with her family. Until she was good and ready.

After the phase in which some of the dying communicate with deceased relatives or spirits, the individual might go into what Dr. Fenwick calls "a different reality," by which he means the person may go toward a vision of brilliant light or toward a sense of love—and also see certain elements or encounters bathed in a kind of hyperlucidity. Dr. Fenwick calls this "a terminal lucidity." This is exactly what the Texas nurse Debbie James witnessed in an 83-year-old patient with a pacemaker in a San Antonio hospital. The patient's name was Helen, and she was in the coronary intensive care unit of which James was manager.

"Helen's in congestive heart failure, and I get to see her all the time," says Debbie James, who likes to use the present tense, as though the patient were still beside her, breathing. "Her color is bad, her lips are blue, but I had to go into surgery just then and I told the other nurses, 'If she starts to go, call me. I'll be there.'"

A little after James returned, she realized Helen was dead. The patient had stopped breathing; she was also DNR—meaning she had left a living will stating that in the event of cardiac arrest, she didn't wish to be resuscitated. When the doctor came in, he looked at the patient's monitor. It was soundless. James told him, "There's no carotid." It had been that way for five minutes, she added.

The cardiologist nodded. He pronounced Helen dead, scribbled it on her chart, and hugged her assembled family, whom he knew pretty well. They all discussed the funeral.

A few moments after the doctor left the room, James heard the kind of breathing that is known in medical circles as "agonal breathing," meaning last gasps. It was coming from Helen's bed.[3] The next sound the nurse heard was a beep from the monitor. Then another beep. Then a third.

"So I am trying to remain calm," James says. But how could she? Helen's adult daughter, also listening to the monitor beeps, was asking, "What's that all about?"

"Ummm . . . it's the heart's last attempt to beat," the nurse replied, struggling for comprehension. She was on occasion privy to certain deathbed oddities: the patient who shouted "MOVE! MOVE! You're in the way," when James knew he wasn't addressing her because she wasn't blocking the path of anyone she could see. The heart attack victim who, after he returned to consciousness, reported having witnessed while he was out his wife and daughter in the emergency room, weeping uncontrollably—and that was exactly what was going on.

In other words, James was quite prepared to accept the unusual. But this beeping sound from a machine monitoring the heart of a dead woman was the oddest moment yet. And it was just the beginning.

Helen's eyelids had started twitching: very much, says James, like an infant's eyelids twitch during REM sleep. Helen's daughter had noticed that as well. And no one understood what was going on. ("Debbie—how do you undocument *deceased?*" another nurse in the room wanted to know.)

"Helen?" James said, addressing the old woman in bed, "where are you, Helen?"

The answer, when it came back, was simple, James recalls: Helen was in a tunnel, she replied, one covered with flowers like the ones her grandmother used to grow. By then her breathing had improved; some color had returned to her face. There was someone with her while she was unconscious, the patient managed to tell the roomful of people. Or rather two someones: Helen's brother, who was by then dead, and another figure, far more familiar to those who didn't know the family.

The old lady mumbled a name. It sounded to the nurse as though Helen had said, "Jesus." In fact, it sounded to her as though Helen was confirming this encounter with Jesus a second time.[4]

If Dr. Fenwick had been in that hospital room right then, he would have immediately diagnosed the situation, calling Helen's Jesus encounter "a deathbed coincidence. And in these you go and see someone with whom you are closely connected and you usually go and tell them you are all right." They generally occur when the individual has stopped breathing, he adds.

Despite all the hoopla that greets each new anecdote reporting an encounter with Jesus or God, they are suspiciously rare among death travelers. Helen's mumbled replies on returning from death may or may not have been a reference to a divine encounter. The old woman with esophageal cancer saw an entire group of invisible beings coming for her. The man with lung cancer spoke with dead relatives, not God. After she died in labor and encountered the wise beings in togas, it never occurred to Jayne Smith to ask if the leader of the group was Jesus or God. It really didn't matter to her. The point was, as far as she was concerned, the leader had answers to those metaphysical questions that needed answering.

In my own research, only two individuals recalled having seen a spiritual being they positively identified as Jesus. One, a pretty Belgian woman, described him in fairly classical terms: "Very much like you see him in the paintings," she explained. "A beautiful face. He wore a long robe."

But most returning death travelers are much more cautious in their identifications of those they either meet or sense nearby. The brilliant light might be "the breath of God," as Pam Reynolds Lowery recalled being told while dead, but she would recall later, it is not God. This is not to suggest a deity is absent during death, or that the reports of a sighting are pure invention. It's simply that the returned are much more likely to feel they were simply in the *presence* of a mystical or unearthly being: In fact, almost half of all of Dr. Greyson's subjects have reported as much.[5]

As for Satan, he seems to be conspicuous by his absence from any death account I've researched—which is, on the whole, very reassuring. More commonly, according to neuropsychiatrist Fenwick, those who come back to life with memories report having met relatives, many of them dead relatives (about a quarter see their parents; 17 percent see siblings). Angels are extremely rare—just 3 percent see those, and in fact, among those I have either interviewed or learned about secondhand from medical personnel, only one, an old woman with end-stage cardiac disease, saw what she assumed to be angels or the characteristics of angels. On the patient's chest sat, briefly, what she described to her nurse Gonzales as "a baby angel."

But the dying woman had been primed to expect as much. Her late husband had always said he would send angels for her "when it was her time," as their daughter phrased it to Gonzales. And indeed, fragments of what seemed like dark wings appeared suddenly at the corners of the old lady's French doors, Gonzales tells me. The nurse herself saw them, she adds. Then, the next day, the dark wings just as abruptly and mysteriously disappeared.

"And do you honestly think," I ask the hospice nurse, "that those dark fragments that seemed like wings were actually angels?"

"Why not?" says Gonzales. "Why not?"

She looks at me with a frank open gaze that seems to say: *Who are we, the living, to decide what or who is coming for us right before or during death? It seems as though pretty much anything can happen.*

In March 1983, David Bennett, a 26-year-old chief engineer of a research vessel, drowned a mile south of Ventura Harbor, off the coast of Santa Barbara. That night there was a massive storm with 25-foot seas, and at some point during the ordeal, Bennett and his limited crew of five had to climb into a rubber Zodiac, which is a sturdy inflatable craft,[6] but not necessarily when it's being pummeled by wave after giant wave. There was a series of these.

"We fell off a 25-footer, just like that—boom!" Bennett recalls. Even when the Zodiac capsized, he didn't panic. He was a trained commercial diver, and in training he had gone through oxygen deprivation exercises, given precisely so that those new to the diving experience wouldn't freak out in a crisis. "Because panic—that's when you die," Bennett explains.

Moreover, the crew had actually brought along life vests, which they absolutely never wore ordinarily. So all in all, Bennett was prepared for rough seas. He wasn't especially worried when he tumbled into the cold, roiling water wearing that extra measure of protection.

Man, I'm really glad we have these on, Bennett thought to himself. He also was thinking a bit about life insurance—was he paid up? But most of all, he felt like a rag doll, flung about by the worst storm he'd ever experienced in his life. The problem was those very life jackets that had first seemed so promising to the crew. Bennett calls them "Mae West life vests" because they bulged like large breasts: Inside they were stuffed with a fluffy pillow filling. In fact, they were old, defective World War II life vests, their fiber filling dry-rotted with age and worse than useless—extremely dangerous to the wearer.

Before Bennett knew it, the fiber lining of his vest was saturated with salt water, pulling him down below the surface of the angry ocean. He struggled in vain, unable to make it back. The rotted vest was his executioner. He had breathed in salt water, he knew that much.

"So I drowned," he says simply.

Drowning was an interesting experience. The engineer found himself in total darkness, surrounded by what he calls without much embellishment "this really rich void." He no longer felt the cold ocean. He felt calm, supported, and best of all, he wasn't being pummeled about by freezing waves anymore.

"Everything was perfect," he says.

"Explain the rich void if you can," I suggest.

"That's the hard part, the explaining," Bennett replies. "But it was this incredible feeling that I was part of the void—and an incredible presence that was also a part of this void and a part of me. It was very comfortable, and yet I had just died this incredibly violent death! But I was not frightened at all. I was just curious. What *was* going on?"

Bennett saw no tunnel, just a point of light. He managed to travel toward it, and as he came closer and closer, he says, he felt "this immense wave of love that was just wrapping me in a warm embrace. It actually felt like it was permeating my being.

"Well, it was pretty obvious that I wasn't in Kansas anymore."

He realized that one way or other, he was in some kind of transition. For him, it was the most natural thing in the world to be wherever it was he was. "There was no distress," is how he puts it, "no concern." He simply felt awed.

Later, much later, Bennett would feel shamefaced about this lack of concern, this carefree evolution from being to nonbeing. He had a wife back home. *Why,* he would later wonder, *was he so unconcerned?*

As he moved toward the brilliant light, part of the answer to that question lay before him. It wasn't just a brilliant spectacle. Inside the luminescence, he realized, were "millions upon millions of fragments of light, and they were all dancing, coalescing, separating, whirling, and moving. And it was beautiful!"

Three fragments of that luminescence broke away. This is the part of his narrative that affects Bennett even now, 20 years after his experience. To my surprise, he begins to cry as he recounts it. The three fragments greeted him, he says, they welcomed him. And he accepted them for who they were or who he thought them to be.

"I recognized them as a family I'd forgotten. I call them my soul family." They were watching him, he realized, even loving him, as he continued to move toward the light.

Growing up, Bennett continues, he'd been without a strong loving and supportive family—although there had been a number of pit stops along the way. "My mother kind of fostered me out on her own," he says drily, "and some of those families were incredibly dysfunctional, and some were abusive or neglectful. So I had this brutal philosophy of life, you just cut your swath in life."

On the other hand, here was this soul family: "They buoyed me up," Bennett continues, wiping away his tears, "until I reached a certain point where the light itself, the infinite light, said *This is not your time, you must go back.*" These were not, he explains, actual words, but he understood the meaning of what the light was trying to convey nonetheless. And he wasn't at all happy about that meaning.

No way I'm going back. I found a family I love, one I never knew I had.

Also, as the young man realized, "I knew my body was cold meat in the ocean. It was in bad shape." He thought he'd produced a remarkably fine argument, cogent and well reasoned, for staying dead. But it didn't work.

You must return. You have a purpose, said the light.

"And when you hear that from something that is infinite consciousness, all-knowing, so much more than ourselves," he says, that's that. You have to come back. "I understood that purpose. And with understanding, I accepted it."

The three fragments of light that had greeted Bennett stayed by him as his body floated closer to the wreckage of the Zodiac. Another giant wave came in, hitting the craft, causing the Zodiac to pop up; as it did so, it pulled Bennett's body, entangled in some of the Zodiac wreckage, to the surface. It also pushed some of the water out of his lungs.

"Then the whole family pushed me back into my body, gently," he says. "And I took a breath."

The other members of Bennett's crew, hearing a squeak and cough coming from the sea, shone a flashlight in his direction: They had somehow or other hung on to that despite the storm. They had been searching for him in the black waters, they later said, for maybe 15 minutes. So that's how Bennett knows how long he had been dead. Bennett hung on to the wreckage of the Zodiac, somehow managing to swim a full mile into shore, his companions beside him. Once on dry land, he surveyed the damage done to him during those minutes when he was knocked down by giant waves. It was pretty severe.

He had a dislocated shoulder. He was ice cold. He was in total shock.

When he finally arrived home, he was wearing only a pair of shorts. There was sand in his pockets, in his ears and eyes. His wife, who happened to be a nurse, touched him: He felt like an icicle. He told her what had just occurred.

"Honey, I think I just died."

She started hitting him, he says. She assumed he was in shock. And besides, Bennett tells me, she herself was in shock. She had just that night fallen asleep and dreamed that her husband was dead.

He couldn't, as things turned out, talk to anyone about the details of his experience. Not to his wife, whom he would ultimately divorce. Nor to his friends.[7] Had he told his story to a psychiatrist, he would have had perhaps a 50-50 chance of getting an interested reception.[8] Above all, he couldn't discuss the experience of drowning with his co-workers, because with the kind of dangerous work Bennett was then involved in, as he explains, commercial diving especially, "The subject of death is taboo."

In fact, he points out, "Any time you have a close brush with death—and we'd had a few—we'd act like guys. You know: bravado, laughing it off. That's why that night of the bad storm, when we finally made it to the beach, there was none of that kind of talk. Nobody said a word. Because we were lucky any of us was alive, and we knew it."

For 11 years, he fought the experience, keeping it "bottled up," as he puts it, and speaking about it to no one. In fact, he found himself barely thinking about it most of the time because, as Bennett puts it, "Logic and reason were the ways I functioned," and the encounter with the three fragments of light he calls his soul family, "didn't fit my engineer brain." Besides, he adds, "I wanted my old life back."

Like most death travelers, Bennett knows there are scientists out there who suspect some voyages are drug induced. I don't ask him about this, even though I figure it's quite possible, given his rocky beginnings, he knows something about the subject. It is Bennett who brings it up, and he's insistent on the subject. "In my early years, I took drugs, and I had LSD flashbacks. Not the same thing. Not even in the same boat," he says vehemently. Those drugged flashbacks he experienced very long ago, he says, were completely disjointed. There was no reality to them.

His old life never came back. It rarely does to those who return from death with memories. What he'd been through the night he was dumped into the freezing ocean could not be explained away by anything he knew of, scientific or otherwise. All he knows, Bennett says, is "This was more real than anything. This was reality."

And it still is, for him. Over a quarter of a century later, those luminous guides he recalls meeting in the angry ocean a mile off Ventura Harbor are—still—his constant companions, the wise, understanding relatives he never had growing up.

Every morning, Bennett greets the day with the same ritual. "I talk to my soul family," he tells me.

CHAPTER SEVEN

WITH OR
WITHOUT GOD

As IT TURNS OUT, it really doesn't matter what you believe. The religion of your parents, the faith you espouse, the God you accept or the God you now, after considerable thought, reject: None of this matters. Something happens when you're dead. That is the only way I can phrase it.

It happens to Christians and Jews, Buddhists and Hindus. It happens whether you believe there's an afterlife, or you disbelieve; whether you believe in God or reject the idea. Death travelers tell me that when they suggest as much at their local churches (often the very ones to which their parents belonged or the churches they attended as children), this message sometimes doesn't go down too well.

"I go to church now because of the church family," Bill Taylor says, meaning the community. "But oftentimes it becomes confrontational with pastors, because most churches preach God has a will for us. There's God up there, and there's us down here. And I say, 'Why do you preach that? Because we're really connected and we're that same energy. Why don't you preach unity or oneness?' But they have to keep to the scripture.

"Nothing wrong with the scripture. But hasn't anything happened since then?"

Interestingly, it is often the nonspiritual, the atheists who think something absolutely has happened.

One bright summer day, I learn as much after I return to the Washington Hospice in Washington, D.C. That's where I used to volunteer years earlier, only by now everything has changed. It is now called the Washington Home and Community Hospices. I greet Tim Cox, its new CEO. He leads me around the place: patients I had never met, a sweet-faced chaplain, unfamiliar nurses and doctors. One of the latter, Katalin Roth, a no-nonsense internist who specializes in palliative care, seems rushed, but she stops when Tim introduces us and shakes hands politely. Until I ask my usual question—"Anyone here you've seen with a near-death experience?"[1] This, she pretty much brushes off with a resounding negative.

Hospice patients, at least those treated in the in-patient unit, are often too sick to talk about anything: They frequently have acute pain or breathing problems. I knew that much from my own experience of volunteering. You'd approach their beds with the simplest questions: Would you like me to read to you? Are you thirsty? They were generally either too weak or too mentally impaired to respond. You'd have to look into their faces to guess their desires, but by a certain point, some of the patients were beyond desiring anything at all.

And besides, Dr. Roth adds when we first meet, she was only working at the hospice part-time. She wears a lot of hats: She is also part of the faculty at George Washington University Medical School, where she teaches geriatrics and medical ethics.

"So I really don't know anyone here who's had a near-death experience," she concludes brusquely. She turns to go, then midway down a corridor, calls out, "Unless you count me. I had one as a kid."

This is the kind of thing that would happen often enough as I conducted my research. An editor who runs a foreign affairs magazine and online blog to which I contribute asked me what kind of book I was writing, and on hearing the reply, said, in an offhand way, "No kidding. I had one of those when I was in college—motorcycle accident. I don't think about it that much." In fact, however, he thinks about it quite a lot, because the next time I saw this editor was at a dinner party (mine, as it happens) and, without prompting, he told an entire roomful of people about his death experience.

But because there's often a spiritual or a religious component to these travels, those listeners without religious affiliation or a belief in a deity tend to dismiss these accounts as prompted by or at least enhanced by faith, mysticism—something with absolutely no scientific basis that did its work on someone with no scientific background. This is why I'm beginning this chapter with Dr. Roth, who is an atheist.

Equally to the point, she was an atheistic child when she peered beyond death's flimsy doors, meaning she was less influenced than most by religious guidance or the teachings of a particular faith. Dr. Roth's parents were a different matter—not only Orthodox Jews, but also Holocaust survivors from Hungary. However, young Katalin, as she tells me, rejected their beliefs out of hand. "I stopped believing in God when I was five," she says flatly. A few years later she was dead. And conscious.

The death and dying experiences of children are similar in many ways to those of adults: The dead often appear to them (mostly grandparents and deceased pets, in the case of children). And above all, the young tend to keep their voyages to themselves for a good long time.

"I didn't tell anyone about my experience until I was 50, and started giving lectures," retired pediatric surgeon Bernie

Siegel tells me. He was four at the time that he choked after aspirating a few plastic pieces of a toy telephone that he had put in his mouth. "Absolutely painful," he adds, "no air coming in." Then, astonishingly, the pain passed, ceasing completely. "I felt totally comfortable; I wasn't in my body anymore," he recalls. "I was up in the air at the head of my bed, watching this kid dying on the bed. I remember the whole dialogue: I thought, *Well my parents are going to find me dead, I feel bad. But I prefer being dead; this is a lot more interesting.*

"I chose death because it was a lot more interesting to be free of everything."

In other words, Dr. Siegel says, "The body was not me. But he [the body] had a seizure,[2] vomited, and the pieces came loose. And the only way I can describe it, is it was like getting caught in a vacuum cleaner. I got sucked back into the body. I had no way of stopping that."

The first words out of his mouth, Dr. Siegel tells me these days, were "Who did that?" "I was mad as hell," Dr. Siegel says. When his mother came into his bedroom, he told her nothing about what had occurred. He was covered with vomit, but mute with anger and betrayal. The airborne adventure that had started off so promisingly was over, switched off by some unseen dispatcher like a television set. Nor is his experience unique. As researcher P. M. H. Atwater discovered, more than three-quarters of the children she interviewed recalled a loving or tranquil start to their journey.[3]

Some 50 years ago, Katalin Roth shared that start. And she was, in her own way, about the least likely child to do so.

She was ten at the time and about to enter sixth grade, when she and her distant cousin Dorian, who was the same age, summered with their respective parents at the Pine View, a now defunct hotel in the Catskills. One hot day, the two girls walked a mile to a big creek, surrounded by a lot of rocks. The creek was perhaps 50 feet wide, the large rocks from which vacationers loved to fish overlooking rushing water.

"I was a bad swimmer," recalls Dr. Roth. "Dorian and I were climbing onto the creek on these rocks, and I hit my head against the rock. I had a concussion and I slipped—and fell into the water. I was out. Unconscious. Well, at the time I thought for just maybe two seconds. But the next thing I knew, I was underwater, and I saw a big white light. A bright, bright light."

Oh, so this is what it's like to die, the child thought. It felt fine, she decided. She felt no fear at all, just "calm and serene. I felt it was very nice."

She has no idea how long she remained in this serene environment of death. She believes she simply blacked out—she didn't see Dorian, her young cousin, pale with fear; she didn't see the onlookers, far away from the swollen current, running around the rocks on the banks of the creek and searching for help. All she knows is that when she came to, there she was, treading water—actually, she amends, "struggling to come up out of the water"—whereas earlier, before the blackout and the white light and the calm feeling, she had definitely not been struggling. More than that, she cannot say. Later that day, she would discover a large gash on her forehead; she had also lost a sneaker. But when her eyes focused on the scene around her, when the bright light subsided, there was Dorian yelling and screaming at her in despair.

"To this day, I can remember it all absolutely clearly, everything," says Dr. Roth. "The people fishing at the creek that day, the rocks, the white light, I saw that white light. I don't know if I told Dorian about that as we walked back to the hotel, me in one sneaker and soaking wet. But I recall it so vividly, it was like a movie."

"Did you tell your parents?" I ask her.

"Are you kidding? I had a hysterical Jewish mother, and the last thing I needed was to tell her and have restrictions on my freedom. NO! I didn't want a worried Jewish mother."

In fact, says the doctor, nothing changed in her life after the drowning. Katalin Roth remained what she was, and always was destined to be: a woman of science and an atheist.

"So this incident didn't make me start believing in God. I don't think this was a religious experience at all. Whatever happens when we die—many people describe the white light, the feeling of peace."

When the interview is over, I reexamine her words, and it occurs to me that the internist clearly feels most comfortable, most reassured defining her experience in a vaster context. If "many people" describe a white light or a sense of peace as their companions during death, these sightings become, if not commonplace, at least nothing exceptional or odd. They place Dr. Roth in the mainstream. The emotions and sighting experienced might be semiprecious stones: beautiful, of course, but not exactly rare.

And in a way, Dr. Roth is right. By now we know that what occurred to her that long-ago summer day was nothing exceptional. Millions have shared it. There is no spiritual component attached to her memories; blissful though the experience was, she doesn't feel it was a gift from heaven or some well-disposed deity. In a way, this is for her a source of tremendous reassurance because it validates what she has thought since childhood: God isn't necessary. We can travel alone.

As it also happens, atheists can be as candid and forthcoming about what occurred while dead as the religious. The Philadelphia neuroscientist Andrew Newberg told me during our interview about one of his acquaintances whom he has written about, also an atheist. Her name is Karen; she is a social worker. "Once while recovering from a hospital procedure, she found herself floating over the nurses' station, where someone was reading a fashion magazine," the neuroscientist reports. "She tried to tell the nurse someone in a bed needed help, but when she looked down, she saw that woman was actually herself—Karen—dying of suffocation. She did recall walking through a tunnel of light at the end of which she saw her deceased uncle, whom she credits with helping her to think critically."

"Go back!" said the uncle. "You still have work to do!"

Karen's next memory was of being revived by a nurse in her hospital bed, Newberg continues. "On her release from the hospital, she concluded that her experience was a purely naturalistic event resulting from oxygen deprivation"—oxygen deprivation being a frequently cited hypothesis to explain the tunnel effect.

Hers was a transcendent event, Karen believed. Most important: It changed her ideas about death and dying. She was no longer afraid of either. She remains a staunch atheist, Newberg writes, her "disbelief in a spiritual realm" unaltered. Like Katalin Roth, she is convinced she traveled alone—traveled light, you might say.

But Karen's belief that oxygen deficiency was responsible for her event begs credulity. As the critical care specialist Dr. Sam Parnia has indicated, those with a lack of oxygen don't have such death experiences. And as Dr. van Lommel and others have concluded, oxygen depletion results not just in heart failure or low blood pressure but also in "confusion and agitation."[4] Death experiences or even near-death experiences, on the contrary, are accompanied by hyperlucidity.

The recollections of the experiences are often tranquil, startling in their wealth of clear, elaborate, ordered detail. Oxygen deprivation as an explanation for what occurs is simply a way of hanging on to an established opinion.

In a similar fashion, Katalin Roth's encounter with death by drowning didn't alter her views: "So do I think because of what I experienced that we're all part of one big spirit? No! I don't," she continues. "And I don't believe in the afterlife. Well—you know, I'm a hard-assed doctor! And I think the white light I saw was probably a neurological reflex."

"But what does that mean exactly?" I wonder.

"A neurological reflex," she repeats. "Beyond that, I don't know." Some months later when we meet again, Dr. Roth will say, "There seems to be some point where the organism is at peace with the process. People ease into it; it's part of what seeing the light does. It's maybe the way the organism responds to the inevitable. In fact, it's probably programmed."

She thinks a bit. "You have no preparation for it, or at least I didn't when I drowned. One moment I was in the present, and the next minute I wasn't."

Then she says exactly what Drs. Parnia and Greyson say at times, and also just about everyone I meet who has traveled while dead: "Something happens."

Ten years ago at a family gathering, Dr. Roth ran into her cousin Dorian once again. They shared a friendly cup of coffee. Then when the cousins were alone, apart from the others, and could speak in private, Dorian told her, "I have never forgotten that day at the creek. You almost died that day." She told Dr. Roth how as a child Katalin had hit her head on a large rock in the creek, rendering her completely unconscious.

Dr. Roth stared in surprise. She'd been underwater for maybe two seconds, she reminded her cousin. She had probably blacked out for a brief moment or so.

"Two seconds?" said the cousin. "No! You were underwater for a few minutes! You didn't come up. Everyone thought you were dead. It was the scariest thing that ever happened. *I* thought you were dead."

Recently, Dr. Roth's husband reminded her that she had told him about the incident, but it was so many years ago that she had quite forgotten she had ever shared the details. In fact, aside from that one confiding moment, it's been her own private buried treasure. She never told her first husband about it, or her friends. "It's just never come up. And I've been in therapy on two different occasions, and I'm sure it's never come up there either," she says. Nor, she adds, did she tell her mentor at Yale Medical School, and she told him a lot because at that point she was a lawyer and she wanted to switch professions.

"Why not?" I prod. "You know, a lot of people with your kind of experience might hide it for a long time, even bury it deep within them, but eventually perhaps they tell friends, mentors, or therapists what happened. Why didn't you?"

"Well, as an adult I thought it was a really important thing that happened to me, because maybe it made me a little more confident in my ability to take care of myself—I like to think it made me braver," says Dr. Roth. "But it was private." After all, death and the nearness of it in the workplace hold no fears for her. "I've been around HIV/AIDS patients, hospice patients—you die," says Dr. Roth with the studied distance of most medical personnel.

"Perhaps," I suggest to Dr. Roth, "you remained silent all these years because you were secretly afraid your listeners, however kindly disposed, might secretly think you're a little crazy?"

She considers this. "If I told people about it—what was the point? Maybe they would think I was crazy," she says finally. "I don't know. Now that I'm talking to you about it, I feel that this is the most conversation I ever had in my life about it."

The next day, she sends me an email. It begins, "It was very good to speak to you about this." And it ends, "I did not realize until we spoke that I had indeed been hesitant to speak about what occurred, partly to avoid seeming odd, and partly because I do pride myself on being a rationalist.

"So thanks for listening."

And yet, there's a bit more to it than that. When I ask Katalin Roth what her death experience meant to her, the bright light, the complete absence of panic in death, she replies after a few seconds of contemplation: "I would say all children think they're different—I had a few secrets, and this one went into the category of this-is-my-own-private-thing-that-sets-me-apart," she replies. "It was a really important thing in my life: I don't think I can explain it."

But after talking to her on two separate occasions, I have another view of how she sees that moment in time she considers strikingly important. I don't think she wants to explain it at all. It would require a rethinking of what life and death are about, which is hard on anyone, but especially for a doctor who takes pride in the description "hard-assed"; it would suggest a reshuffling of who we all are in the universe and what we may expect. It's a tough thing to reexamine previous beliefs and lay oneself open to completely different conclusions. For myself, I happen to know that all too well.

Because, I realize as I write this book, I have spent almost my entire life being wrong. And sometimes you can reconcile what you think now with what you thought before. But in this instance, you cannot.

And another issue is: Do these experiences, the ones affecting both believers and atheists, truly match up? Is the atheist's experience empty of God perhaps a good deal less compelling than the death recollections of a religious person? When we come down to it, is that the atheist's real "punishment" for denying God—a less spectacular voyage? And conversely, are the devout more likely to get a better class of accommodations, more impressive insights and metaphysical encounters than nonbelievers?

The answer is: Probably not. If there's one thing that's likely, given the anecdote that's about to follow, it's that believers and nonbelievers go through similar portals into similar worlds, and often return with similar recollections. How they interpret those travels in this world once they come back—therein lies the difference.

Like Katalin Roth, Joseph Robidoux was a bad swimmer when he was young. He knew it, and yet he chose to ignore it. At 19, he went swimming with a group of friends in a large lake right outside of Halifax. Back then he was a gentle, sweet-faced boy from the town of Fredericton in New Brunswick, Canada. Raised Catholic, he was a church regular. Despite his drawbacks, young Joseph in those days had the kind of trust in his capable friends who swam well, and in himself, that most of us don't have.

Among other things: Joseph trusted that he could swim to a specific rock his friends had singled out as a kind of initial landing site where he could catch his breath. "But I couldn't get my footing on that rock," Robidoux recalls. He tried swimming to yet another rock, but he never did make it.

"And then I went under, it was just—depth," he says. "Everything kind of goes black on you." *So this was the end,* he decided. At the time, he was completely unaware that all around him were his swimming buddies.

"The first thing I remember was feeling very sorry for my parents, for the grief that they would experience on learning I was dead," he continues. "I was the oldest of four children, and I knew how unhappy they would be."

Desperately, he tried to summon the words of a traditional Catholic prayer that is recited at life's end. At first the simple words refused to come to him, but after much struggle they somehow or other seeped into his mind: "Into your hands O Lord I commend my spirit." Those were the last words of Christ. And they were also the last words of Mary, Queen of Scots, before her execution.

As he repeated those words of complete comprehension and submission, the teenager found himself moving toward a white light that illuminated the end of a long rectangular corridor. Like young Katalin Roth, Joseph felt nothing but joy when he considered that bright light. At the same time, he felt another source of elation: The words for which he had struggled hard had in fact finally come to him. They had been given to him as a last gift, he decided. It was, he concludes, "an experience of love."

In death he saw no one, however. Not Jesus. Not a dear relative, deceased or otherwise. And then the experience was over. Someone was pulling him out of the water.

"I remember feeling so sad," he tells me, "because this wonderful movement toward the light was being interrupted. I couldn't go there. I didn't want to go back."

He would never tell his parents about the incident, not at 19 and not ever. "It was a deeply personal thing," he tells me. "Maybe it would have frightened them to know I was so close to death." He doesn't recall telling the friends with whom he was swimming about what he saw, either. Perhaps just a dozen people in his life know about his movement toward the light, he says.

"I wonder if the experience of drowning and seeing the bright light had something to do with your becoming a monk," I tell him. *Maybe a great deal to do with it,* is what I'm actually thinking.

Because after many of life's detours, that's who Robidoux is these days. At 61, the same age as Dr. Roth as it happens, he is Brother Dunstan, dressed in a monk's long dark robe, his round bespectacled face still with reflection. He lives in great simplicity in northeast Washington, D.C., where he heads the Lonergan Institute and examines theological and philosophical matters. In fact, when we speak, it is in the deep quiet of a hot July evening at St. Anselm's Abbey, after a simple supper at the refectory.

We are sitting on small stuffed couches in the tiny Victorian parlor of the lovely old building, which is fronted by stained glass and gray stone. It is the perfect venue for asking about life after drowning, and the interesting series of choices that followed a long-ago death. It is an ideal moment to speculate on whether dying and then returning might provoke a drastic change of obligations, beliefs, and duties.

Brother Dunstan laughs and says, "Holy Moses! Only in a kind of subterranean way that I can't definitively identify.

"You know, I never actually stopped practicing the faith or going to mass," he continues, "but for many years I lived as a kind of practical atheist. Oh sure, I would observe the forms of religious observance, but whether or not I was actually living this life—the life I was called to—is a different question. Because anybody who's had any kind of religious upbringing can easily for many years live the *form* of it.

"But it's only when life's crises come that maybe all this stuff might mean something."

Some years after the drowning incident, Robidoux entered the Jesuit novitiate, which he did for two years. Eventually, however, he would discard that path, feeling he simply wasn't cut out to be a Jesuit.

"Have you ever wanted to repeat your death experience?" I wonder.

"Oh yes, it would be a wonderful thing at the end of my life to go to that light in a joyful, loving way," he replies swiftly. Then, "But you know, the thing is, Judy, we don't know how we're going to end up."

Brother Dunstan explains. On the one hand, he says, as a Catholic you're not supposed to assume automatically that you're going to make it, that salvation, God, the long corridor leading to jubilation and a brilliant light, will be yours when you die. "One cannot be presumptuous," is how the monk puts it. And many men in this world, he adds, are in fact very presumptuous.

"You know men can be SOBs," he observes.

Whereas most women, the monk adds, are just the opposite of men in the way they view death. They tend to be despairing about their chances for joy or salvation when the end comes. Brother Dunstan isn't the only one who has observed this interesting pattern, he adds. John Swain, the Canadian onetime acting director of the world's Jesuit Order, once told him much the same thing: There is a distinct difference between the assumptions of women and men regarding their likelihood of attaining post-life bliss and salvation. Women tend to be pessimistic, he says. And they shouldn't be. No one should be.

A few months after our first meeting, Brother Dunstan was called to the deathbed of a relative who was dying of cancer and very afraid, as the relative told his visitor. That was when Brother Dunstan told him about his own experience drowning at 19, and extrapolated from that incident in order to soothe the sick man.

"When you die, you never lose consciousness," he comforted his relative. "You always remain conscious. You know in this life, no matter how good it is, no matter how well things are going for you, you are never completely satisfied. There's always something missing, although we just don't know what it is, we just know we aren't satisfied with what's happening. But when you die, where you end up going—it's home. And you know it's home."

"And did your dying relative feel comforted as he listened to the details of your own death experience?" I ask Brother Dunstan.

"Yes, I believe he did. There were tears in everyone's eyes after I told my story, tears in his eyes too," says the monk. Then, "So my point is, we should always be hopeful."

And yet—here Brother Dunstan's voice descends to a murmur—he understands the gloomy view of death held by so many women. He understands despair more than he would like to. Because when I ask him if he believes he will see the face of God or Jesus at life's end, this is what he says: "Judy, I honestly tend to be despairing. This may seem strange. I cannot be presumptuous that I am going to make it. I tend to think that I cannot make it. I look at all my feelings and—oh my goodness—how could I possibly be accepted into God's Kingdom?

"That's how I feel," the monk continues. "And I don't have a completely satisfactory explanation for that."

"But Brother Dunstan," I protest, "how can you despair? Especially since at 19 you experienced bliss and the bright light, the all-encompassing happiness you felt when you died. You've been there.

"Clearly," I suggest, "somebody once liked you enough to show you what's in store for you the next time around."

Brother Dunstan does not appear to be convinced, however.

"My experience—it was a grace," he replies simply. "It's a mystery to me. It's just a complete mystery. But it was a beautiful gift."

Sometimes, I imagine, that's all a death travel is on the surface: a complete mystery. A grace. "An experience of love," as the monk puts it. But unlike other mysteries and gifts, it is an experience that stays with you, whether or not you choose to acknowledge its influence. It stayed with Katalin Roth, even though generally she chooses not to discuss it for fear of being thought irrational—about the worst thing a physician can be. It stayed with Brother Dunstan, even though he honestly wonders whether the grace and the mystery will be there waiting for him the next time he dies.

And yet—here is the paradox: For years, neither the monk nor the doctor was anxious to reveal to many people, often the people closest to them, what occurred. They kept what they had learned for the most part inside themselves, because, no matter how important or gratifying their discoveries, the revelation would have altered the opinions of those who thought they knew them. Everything would be questioned: the quality of their work, their intelligence, their sanity. Thus, a physician felt she couldn't tell her story to fragile patients who might have taken comfort from her recollections. And a man of God felt for a long while reluctant to speak of that form of grace.

I think Brother Dunstan is on to something when he suggests that these extraordinary travels may well be the answer to the "something missing" in our lives, the reason why, no matter how good things seem to be, most of us are never quite satisfied. After the return, the memory—for those lucky enough to have a memory—is ever present. It informs what you do, who you are at your core, the choices you make, whom you tell about what happened, and whom you refuse to tell or neglect to tell. It is what makes you different, or rather, seemingly different from the rest of humanity. Why else would Brother Dunstan, who has told so few people about what occurred long ago back in that lake, have nonetheless summoned his story as a source of consolation at the deathbed of a dying relative? Why else did he explain to that relative that he now knows consciousness endures, really forever?

Why would he have told me about it?

Most important of all: Why would he have described his encounter with the brilliant light, the intense love he says he felt in the afterlife, in the exact words of so many of those who have returned from the dead? "It's home," Brother Dunstan says flatly, "and you know it's home." This is not some accidental choice of verbiage—or rather, it might be accidental on the monk's part, but it is a perfect echo. Going home, Dr. Greyson tells me approvingly very early on, is precisely the phrase used by many travelers to describe their voyages beyond the border.

"They say, 'I went back to where I belong,' " Dr. Greyson explains during our first talk. "They say 'That's home.'"

However, what the encounter with the light doesn't necessarily guarantee is a lifetime of happiness. It doesn't necessarily mean things will be easy on the voyager after his return. Just . . . different. Enlightenment carries a cost. And the monk knows that as well.

"Happy?" Brother Dunstan echoes. "I guess so, you know. I had to force myself to come here in the end, to go through with it. But I came. I stayed. One day at a time, as they say in Al-Anon or Alcoholics Anonymous. What I've been doing is postponing my departure for years. Because we live in a broken world, we are not in charge.

"But regardless of how bad things might be on a given day, I am going to celebrate," Brother Dunstan concludes. Then he repeats a certain phrase once again, and despite all his anxiety and all his pain, I think he means what he says from the bottom of his gentle doubt-filled heart: "It has been a great blessing."

The blessing, The Knowing, the bright light, the contemplative music, the wise strangers on a faraway hill, the dark block of stone that is really a temple, the luminous threads that connect every portion of the universe: I am not sure they are all the same thing, differently interpreted, but they are all part of the after-death, the welcome committee standing on the bank of the River Styx. They are all on tap to the religious, the unreligious, the scoffers, the believers, the confused, and the doubtful. How long they stay with us after our hearts and brains shut down—that no one knows for sure. But for a while anyway, they are there, offering a few answers to questions that plague the living. We are not alone. We will not be left alone. The puzzling dissatisfaction so many of us feel in life is answerable in death. We will, one day or another, one way or another, all be going home. And, as Brother Dunstan suggests, when we finally arrive, we will know for sure that it's home.

CHAPTER EIGHT

UNASKED-FOR GIFTS: THE KNOWING AND THE POWERS

FOR YEARS DAVID BENNETT, who drowned in 25-foot waves during a fierce storm off Ventura Harbor and then recovered from death, told no one aside from his wife about his experience. He kept it all to himself, although eventually to no avail. Certain elements marked him, he felt, as a changed person, a man altered in uncanny ways unavailable to most of those who had never died.

"I started to have intuitive knowings," he says. "I didn't know where this information came from. All sorts of things, personal information about co-workers, engineering things, failures, all kinds of things—suddenly I would know things. These intuitive knowings—they were like I'd already discussed them with somebody. It was very strange." He will not be more specific. He is a modest man, and also a cautious one.

But much of what Bennett sensed had nothing to do with the secret lives and career failings of colleagues. Part of what he came to know occurred, says Bennett, during a death passage that is known in experiencer circles as "a life review."

The life review occurs to certain of the dead after they have moved past the light of tranquillity and acceptance. During it, they encounter what Raymond Moody describes as "a detailed review of everything they have done in their lives." It is among the rarest elements of a classic death experience. In their article in *The Lancet* detailing a study of 344 cardiac arrest patients in ten Dutch hospitals, for instance, Dr. van Lommel and his associates cite "life review" in few of the 62 patients who reported "some recollection of the time of clinical death." Far more common in their experiences, according to the patients themselves, are other sensations: "an awareness of being dead"—half of all clinically dead patients knew that much—and "positive emotions," which 56 percent reported. Almost 30 percent saw a celestial landscape; almost a quarter believed they had communicated with the light. But only eight—roughly 15 percent—experienced a life review.

There is a general feeling among the resuscitated that life reviews come, if they come at all, only toward the end of a relatively lengthy death passage. Sophisticated cardiopulmonary resuscitation swiftly administered may save a life, but it can also curtail (or even prevent) a full life review. "I had a brief life review, just the high and low points but no details," the surgeon Anthony Cicoria, who was struck by lightning in upstate New York, tells me. "I've read that a lot of people have that—a brief review. But if you're out there long enough, then it goes into the more in-depth review."

David Bennett's was pretty in-depth, and like most life reviews, involved certain elements that were neither blissful nor congratulatory.

"I relived my life not only from my own point of view but from the point of view of everyone with whom I'd ever interacted," is how he describes it. "And not only was I experiencing it, but my entire soul family were all experiencing it in the same way," he adds, referring to the fragments of light he viewed while drowning. It was these fragments of light, the ones that turned into actual beings, that "somehow became the family I'd forgotten I had."

Because of his rough upbringing, tossed about from one family to the next, as he describes it, Bennett had been until his death, "self-centered," he says, "with a survivalist mentality." That was who he was as a young man, and he didn't think much about it.

But during his life review, he says, he was forced to recall a specific scene of which he was deeply ashamed.

"A guy approached me in a bar when I was living in Sedona; it was a cowboy bar," he says. "I beat the living you-know-what out of him because he approached me sexually." This apparently stray moment appeared in Bennett's life review. "And it was a very strange occurrence," he continues. "Because I not only felt my rage, but I felt his shame. And I felt the bartender's irritation at the whole situation. And I felt how the other patrons at the bar felt about this guy who started a brawl, their anger and their angst. It was palpable.

"So my soul family had to experience some of that, and I was ashamed at some of the things I had done, the people I had hurt. I saw the ripples of my actions."

Some of these ripples came from actions that were good and decent. "I realized how when I did something with loving intention, it created the biggest ripple," he says. "What I thought was important in life, like becoming a chief engineer, things I had a lot of pride in, had very little far-reaching ripple significance. But loving interactions— I saw how important all that was.

"Emotions are so much different there," he continues. "My soul family—if I can say anything about their emotions—they were excited because they were honored to be a part of my life review. That was all crystal clear."

For Bennett, sensing the feelings of others was a gift he carried back with him into life. Other travelers also return with heightened intuitive capabilities. Clairvoyance, ESP, curative powers: All these are cited by some of the returning dead and in the studies based on their accounts conducted by scientists and physicians.

Some of these surprising gifts and acquisitions are of the prosaic but very gratifying variety. The British neuropsychiatrist Peter Fenwick, for example, had an extremely intelligent patient, an air traffic controller, who after a death experience became astonishingly good at predicting the movements of the stock market—much to Fenwick's amusement, because he failed to follow up on his patient's suggestion to buy British Telecom, which promptly soared.

But more often, these sudden endowments are inexplicable and arcane, the kind that Dr. van Lommel carefully identifies in his book *Consciousness Beyond Life: The Science of the Near-Death Experience*. Among those gifts cited: clairvoyance, telepathy, precognition, déjà vu, healing ability, spirits, and out-of-body experiences.[1] He calls such powers "enhanced intuitive sensitivity." Indeed, Dr. van Lommel writes, between 84 and 92 percent "feel inundated with information from or via another dimension," accounting for the majority of the returning dead. And those who return are not necessarily overjoyed, he adds, to be thus endowed: "Clairvoyance, enhanced sensitivity, and precognition can feel extremely threatening," he suggests.[2]

"I would say an NDE can be very positive, but it is a trauma, such a trauma!" Dr. van Lommel tells me when we meet in the Netherlands. "You see, it's a hard struggle. It's a spiritual crisis. It takes years and years to accept it. And then years and years to interpret it. And you have an enormous responsibility about the information you receive."

Small wonder then that some of the formerly dead return determined to volunteer no mention of such extraordinary abilities or insights, either to friends or researchers. In fact, many have to be asked specifically about a possible acquisition of enhanced sensitivity before offering a response.

It is Dr. van Lommel's opinion that the new unasked-for gifts are the results of the death experience itself. "I think the NDE changes the function of your body and perhaps even the function of your DNA," he says. The people who are newly endowed, he has observed, "can know future events, details of life to come. The past and the future are available, because there's no time, no distance, and no space. But they don't discuss it because people don't believe it."

Given the right environment, though, as I have found, certain travelers—the ones who have found acceptance, and almost always the ones whose experiences occurred years previously—jump at the chance to discuss their new gifts. The hallways and rented ballrooms at IANDS conferences throng with the returned, offering seminars, curative sessions, or methods for contacting spiritual guides. The return from death, some of them feel, has endowed them with special powers.

Many of these claims of curative touches I find hard to believe. ("It's not about belief, because I have seen it—for me it's about seeing and then trying to understand," Dr. van Lommel warns me in his calm way when I question the vaunted curative powers of certain returning travelers.)

And it is true that Pam Reynolds Lowery showed special, absolutely inexplicable gifts in that area: She roused a hospitalized boy in Savannah, his lungs burned by chlorine, and she pulled another young man, this one comatose, back to consciousness with a whispered joke about bad hospital food and pizza. Pam's daughter Michelle tells me that her mother didn't even have to touch her leg to cure an occasional childhood ache: Pam used Reiki, a Japanese spiritual practice that can aid in healing.

But Pam had, as her husband, Butch, told me, "perceptions well before her brain aneurysm surgery as well as after."

One day during their early years together, Butch says, while his wife was still a healthy and vital young woman, the two of them went shopping for groceries. As they stood in the checkout line, Butch found Pam acting, as he puts it, "very weird." She was visibly distressed.

"What's going on?" Butch asked his wife.

"The lady in front of us—she just lost someone close to her," Pam replied.

No way, Butch thought to himself. He was still new to his wife's intuitive abilities, and unsure of what to make of them. He found himself tapping the woman in front of them in line, and pursuing his wife's hunch: "Was there a recent death," he asked the woman in line, "possibly one that deeply affected you?"

The result, he adds, was horrifying. "How do you know that?" the woman asked.

"Because my wife just told me."

"But I don't know you people!" said the woman in line, and she started weeping.

"And of course it got worse after the surgery—Pam's perceptions," Butch says. That's when The Knowing, as she called it, descended.

When I recount the traumatic effects of Pam's reported ability to absorb the thoughts of strangers to Pim van Lommel, he is not in the least surprised. He knows the syndrome. In his experience, he says, hundreds of people who have endured a temporary death have recounted the same sort of aptitude.

Still, my skepticism about the sudden endowments of death experiencers is hard to brush aside.

"The danger is people get so inflated," says Nancy Evans Bush, whose terrifying voyage during death puts her at odds with the more blissful experiencers around us at the IANDS gathering when we first meet. "I even met one person who said, 'Oh, but I can't expect you to understand, because my consciousness is higher than your consciousness.'" She smiles at the recollection, but it is a wry smile, her face set and mirthless.

So although I am far from dismissing reports of the heightened sensitivity that seems to crown so many of the returning dead—like van Lommel—I suspect death does indeed have a way of altering cellular interaction and perhaps our DNA; it would be very strange if it didn't—I also think we have to be cautious about our conclusions. Those like Pam Reynolds Lowery, who already were endowed with certain extrasensory abilities before briefly dying, found their powers increased after death. But perhaps the more striking incidents of enhanced perception come from those who say they had never before experienced psychic powers, visions, or paranormal sensibilities until after they returned from the dead.

Decades after her death journey, Jayne Smith found herself at a seven-day meditation workshop conducted by the American spiritual leader Ram Dass.[3] Gazing at him, she says, she saw a striking series of changes on his face that seemed to reassemble into an old acquaintance: the tall pale man in the toga with the fringe of white hair she had met in her travels years earlier. "And I saw that my spiritual authority, whoever it was, had managed to transmit his face," she recalls. "Then I shut my eyes and opened them. Looked again. Gone. The face of my spiritual adviser was gone. He never came again. But while he was there, my heart stopped."

To returned travelers, these psychic gifts can also provide a form of wordless communication, an ability to know things that by rights should remain unknowable—often the facility, without asking a single question or uttering a syllable, to recognize others who have died.

"It was from their eyes that I could tell if a person had a near-death experience," Bill Taylor, who endured three successive cardiac arrests, informs me about those he met when he attended his first IANDS conference years ago.

"Going to that conference, I knew no one there; I went with no one," he continues. "You're walking in the door not knowing anybody. And I realized I could tell who was sitting next to me in the room.

"I would say, 'Oh, are you an experiencer?' and they would say, 'Oh yes, I am.' I would say, 'Are you a researcher?' And they would say, 'Yes, I am.' There's an—I don't know—a terrific communication in the eyes. And then it extends to movements, to tone of voice, everything. But the eyes were very clear. And I remember going up to people, and saying, 'Could I just look into your eyes?' There's a loving energy there."

But, Taylor adds, he was able to do more than simply recognize the like-minded voyager. He recalls, at the same conference, meeting an older man who was discussing his dead wife.

"And I immediately had the feeling: *His wife wants me to tell him she's all right, and she sends him her love*," he says. "So I did that. The guy was in tears. And I said, 'I don't know where this is coming from, I don't hear it audibly. But it's just very strong that she's here and she wants me to tell you that.'

"That happens once in a while. Not very often," Taylor says, half apologetically. "Whereas before the NDE I would never have had those experiences. It just opens that door."

For David Bennett, the door swung open as his body lay lifeless, buffeted about in the freezing ocean. That, he says, is when another realization came through clear enough: He was going to get cancer some day or other.

"I didn't know it at the time, but I was seeing the future," Bennett explains.

Bennett got a divorce, as so many do who have experienced a death event. He turned, as so many also do, to the community of fellow experiencers, seeking what he calls "mentors and near-death experiencers to help me face this and get through this." He began to see, he says, that there was no getting rid of what he had gone through, "that my NDE was implanted in my being," and now that it refused to be repressed, now that it had emerged to the fore, he had to do something about it.

Mainly, Bennett decided, he had to start changing his life.

And that's just what he did, Bennett continues. He abandoned his life in California as a chief engineer of an ocean research vessel; he no longer wanted to pursue a life at sea. He moved to upstate New York and changed jobs—radically.

"I became the manager of a dialysis program because I wanted to be of service," he recalls. "This incredible urge to be of service was overwhelming me."

In November 2000, he was sitting in his dialysis office in Syracuse, New York, when, he says, he felt "like my back exploded." He went to the emergency room of St. Joseph's Hospital, underwent x-rays, and that's how Bennett found out that he had lung cancer. It had metastasized, he says, to his spine. "And my spine had collapsed," he explains.

In other words, as his life review 16 years earlier had prophesied, he did indeed have cancer. Stage 4 lung cancer, says Bennett. He was 43 at the time of diagnosis.

"And they found lesions in my hip, my brain, and my kidney, and they told me at the hospital that they were going to make me as comfortable as possible with morphine and Percocet," he recalls. "And that I should get my affairs in order. That I had only about six to eight weeks to live. It was in my bones."

"And did you get your affairs in order?" I wonder.

"No. Because I had seen long before in my life review in my death experience that I was going to get cancer and survive," Bennett replies. "The spirit family guided me to use traditional as well as holistic approaches—chemotherapy and radiation, too, all at the same time. The spirit communication taught me how to mindfully encapsulate the pain so I could live my life."

Then Bennett says, almost casually, "The five-year prognosis of survivability was one-tenth of one percent."

And while he is talking, I know what Bennett will say next. Because the neuropsychiatrist Peter Fenwick, who doesn't know Bennett at all, has already apprised me: "This is one of the things we know about NDEs," he says. "People come back healed."

We are talking to each other, Bennett and I, a good dozen years after his grim prognosis. And I don't want to make too much of Dr. Fenwick's conclusions—I don't want to suggest for a moment that once you've had an experience, all will be cured. Because since his diagnosis, Bennett has had three spine surgeries. Also, to be honest, I have no idea what he means by his ability "to mindfully encapsulate the pain," of which the guy clearly has had a lot. I don't know what the phrase really suggests or involves. Especially since Bennett also says, "The chemo—oh my God! It's worse than the cancer! It's horrendous."

I ask him, "Why, if you were told by certain fragments of light, this spirit family, as you call it, that you would someday get metastatic cancer but survive, did you decide to go through the horrors of chemotherapy and radiation? Why not leave your body alone and trust to the prophecy?"

At that, he laughs. "Because of my purpose," says Bennett. And then he repeats, "Because of my purpose." His spirit family told him, he says, that once he recovered from cancer, he would be in a position to help other patients with the illness, and he would also be able to talk to and counsel those who had been through death and returned.

"I am working with experiencers all over the world now," Bennett explains. "I don't want others to experience the isolation that I had. So a lot of my purpose is working with experiencers, to help them get through the integration period. And it seems I am always helping, and also mentoring one or two terminally ill patients."

He is cancer-free, just as predicted, he says. Nonetheless, he goes for regular checkups to the oncologist.

"And when you go, you have that natural human thing, that angst," he concedes. "Every time you go for a checkup, in the back of your mind, you know it's there, it's playing these little games with you. *WHAT IF?* It's a natural thing. You kind of dread these checkups."

"I want to live in a connected house with nearby neighbors," a death traveler I visit tells me practically the minute I set foot in her living room. "Not a solitary stand-alone house because I'm living alone." In the course of our subsequent conversation, this woman also tells me what her particularly joyful death experience has taught her: "I know now there's a plan for us all, and that plan is beautiful and full of love." In fact, she says, "I would say that sometimes we're wasting our time worrying about stuff."

So you cannot help asking such a person, a death experiencer who has learned through her encounter that there's a beautiful, loving, and logical plan for us all, and who has also learned that there is no need to worry about whatever bothers us in life: Why insist on living in a connected house with neighbors close by? Why entertain any fears at all about incidents ugly or even fatal that might happen while living alone? After all, a well-ordered, structured universe is just that—the embrace of all those who reside there. Fate is not a matter of accident in this scenario. Why not go with the flow?

"That's a good question," this woman concedes. "I consider safety because I'm a human being. It's that simple. I would have gone back to death immediately after the experience was over—and for several months after that experience, I would also have gone back.

"But then you get involved with life again and your family, whom you love. And you think, *OK, I am willing to wait.* I love life, I have great friends, so why would I want to do anything that might get me out of here more quickly? I know I am safe in the universe. I also know I'm not ready to go.

"And probably that doesn't make any sense either," she concedes with a shrug.

And she's right. Nothing this woman who worries about her safety has said makes a lot of sense, and yet at the same time, everything she's said is shared by those I've interviewed. Every last person. In death, most of them wish to stay right where they are: dead. In life, they want just as forcefully to cling to life.

As it turns out, no matter how arresting, uplifting, or transcendent the voyages, the brutal *What if?*—the implacable sense that death is something objectionable, a state to be resisted for as long as possible—never quite goes away. A large number of the formerly dead report the same schism: a stark emotional divide between what they know from experience and what they wish to stave off despite experience. And of course, the two responses to self-preservation don't line up at all. The inbred, instinctive human reaction to the prospect of death cannot, it would seem, be thoroughly scrubbed. It can be alleviated to an admirable, even an enviable, extent, as those I have interviewed report. They are the ones who have experienced death and found it (most of them, anyway) very much to their liking. So the terror of the final moment recedes. But the urge to postpone, and postpone it for as long as possible, never does.

∞

This was brought home to me with special emphasis after my internist—the very internist who had told me two years earlier that she found the subject of death travels fascinating but knew no one with such memories—interrupted my latest checkup with a piece of news.

"Are you still working on your book?" she wondered. "Because I can't stop thinking about the subject matter. And also I may have someone for you—a patient who says she will speak to you."

In 2013, while riding in a car, Maryland artist Glenna Park tells me, she experienced a heart attack, and subsequently the absorbing spectacle of watching what she calls "the ghost of myself" emerge from her own body. It was almost like a snakeskin in its ease of release, she says at one point. At another, she describes the ghostly emergence this way: "I saw it sliding off over my head like when you take off a shirt."

Immediately, she adds, the thought came to her: *I am dying*. But there was no panic. "My sense of color diminished, a gray fog came over me. But I wasn't alarmed."

If the prospect of the end didn't alarm her, it was because she had met death before, always without fear. She has a history of heart attacks, and has also undergone out-of-body experiences, "which I don't usually tell people about, because they think it's weird," she adds.

Also, decades earlier, when she was 15, Park drowned and experienced the same reassuring welcome as Katalin Roth and Brother Dunstan—but with a twist: "A long gold light," she recalls. "I somehow came out of a tunnel in which it seemed like a bunch of movies were all playing at the same time and then into this really warm, most perfect sunlight." In other words, Park is strong in her conviction that, as she flatly asserts, "There is absolutely life after life, but in a different form. And last time around, I kind of moved on to another form of existence, the one that would last forever."

However, she is in no hurry either to reacquire that new form on a permanent basis. "Death is not first on my immediate list of things to do," Park observes drily. "I haven't done everything I want to do."

In other words, the Darwinian push for survival, the instinctual hunger for an extended life from extinction, often despite enormous pain, is as potent a force as the existential knowledge obtained by those who return—the ones who know that the last breath isn't equivalent to the last second of consciousness. And those two opposites—the instinct and the experience—are irreconcilable combatants. Yet in this world, in these travelers, they coexist.

By chance, I come across one person who makes use of certain Darwinian explanations for the more sanguine experiences of the returned—and yet at other moments feels strongly that in some sense the dead do return, however briefly. She is a nurse, a woman of science, and is initially fairly reluctant to speak about an incident she clearly considers important.

She tells me straightaway when we meet, for instance, that she does not really believe that whatever these people recall, the blissful memories especially, are actually voyages through death.

"They're caused by hypoxia," is her analysis. "You know, low oxygen. It's sort of like when people are choked. The lack of oxygen to the brain creates this feeling of well-being." And when I suggest, as I seem to be doing frequently to scoffers, that low oxygen actually decreases the mind's ability to remember events—and especially minimizes or annihilates the brain's ability to absorb and then recall events in the orderly and vivid way so many of the returning dead manage to do—she retreats with a hasty, "Hmmm. I think you're right."

And that's that. The nurse, whose name is Gerry Rebach, evidently doesn't want to get into an argument, that much is clear. But it's also obvious that her opinion of these experiences hasn't changed. She believes the comforting recollections of the returning dead to be part of a biological design, nature's trick to ease the process of leaving. "I always thought that something natural occurs within the individual that makes it OK to die," she explains. "Death is something I see as programmed."

She herself has never died. But as we talk over coffee, I come to learn that she was visited by someone who did die, and then tugged at her sleeve.

Some two years ago, Gerry Rebach begins, she was lying in her bed on a Monday morning, "in a twilight state," as she puts it, not thinking of much that was important. She was calm, thoughtful, unprepared for what came next.

"And then I felt totally enveloped by literally a transparent golden bubble, and this feeling of complete peace," she recalls. "And I saw a friend's face, just sort of smiling. He never said anything. There was no agitation in his face. There was just this enveloping presence, this enveloping vision of his face in front of me."

He was a very close friend, she adds, a teacher. The two talked often. During the course of the ensuing day, she discarded that image of her smiling friend and the enveloping gold bubble in which she had been briefly enclosed and paid it no further mind. Still it was odd, she feels in retrospect. Nothing like that vision or that image had ever appeared to her. Not before or since.

Four days later she learned that her close friend had died, very suddenly. "He wasn't ill," says the nurse. "Not that anyone knew, anyway. But his son found him in his apartment with a cold compress on his head. He'd had a heart attack." She feels very sure, she adds, about one thing: It was no accident that while lying in bed that Monday morning she saw her friend's face. "I really came to believe that was the hour of his death," she says.

As it turns out, Pim van Lommel is familiar with this sort of parting note from the deceased. "When somebody's presence is sensed at a moment when this person's death is still unknown," he writes, "we speak of a perimortem experience." It is only later, the doctor adds, that the news of the death emerges. And it is evidently not an uncommon experience. Researchers at Tilburg University in the Netherlands asked just such a question of respondents: Had they ever had contact with someone who was dead? Among American respondents, all anonymous, 30 percent replied they had had such contact. Among Europeans, the number was slightly lower: 25 percent.

So Gerry Rebach's moment with the smiling face of her dead friend, her perimortem experience, although unusual as far as she is concerned, has already been examined and categorized. Dr. van Lommel would not be surprised to hear about it. Gerry Rebach, on the other hand, cannot get over it.

"I just feel very strongly he had come to say goodbye, that this is why I saw him, smiling," she continues. "Although he never said anything to me, that image was with me. Because it wasn't an action sequence like most dreams are. It was this enveloping feeling of peace."

"Whose peace?" I wonder. "Yours or his?"

"My feeling of peace and his peace," replies the nurse. "Both."

By the time I see Bruce Greyson yet again, a year has passed, and peace, as far as I'm concerned, is in short supply. My mother is near death, not that I know this for an absolute fact on the summer day that I drive down to Virginia. Or if

I do suspect it—she has broken her hip, at her advanced age generally a precursor to even worse issues, and she is also thinner than before; her appetite is not the raging force it was just a few months earlier—I choose not to think about it. With Dr. Greyson, I prefer to talk about the people we both now know or the people we wish we had known: Nancy Evans Bush, Bill Taylor, Tony Cicoria, and Pam Reynolds Lowery, the ones who died and came back, whose death changed them in some significant and essential way. Like Dr. Greyson himself, who told me at the end of our first talk that his work has changed him substantially.

"In what way?" I wondered.

Greyson replied: "I'm no longer as afraid of death as I used to be."

Like me, for that matter, I think during the second drive down to his office. I too am no longer as afraid. Generally. Often.

In fact, I am feeling very much at ease with the subject that used to be, for me anyway, a source of utter incomprehension and dread. For decades, it had been one of the very few characteristics I shared with my mother, who was the queen of fear. In our house the most banal questions on the subject—*Do you want cremation or a burial? Do you want to give that family ring to my sister now rather than, say, when you are 98?*—were taboo. As though the mere act of discussion might be the vehicle to bring it all to a close. When I visit, I want to comfort her with what

I've learned while researching this book. But Alzheimer's is a tricky business, a mean bouncer: It doesn't usually allow outsiders entrance. And even if it does on rare occasions, anything that does manage to penetrate gets mangled along the way.

So for the sake of my mother, who can no longer ask anything at all, I decide to ask the psychiatrist what I promised myself early on in this odyssey of death I would never ask again, namely whether Greyson believes that what the people I've interviewed (some of whom he recommended I see) say they experienced while dead really did happen to them—by which I mean happened to them in a direct, physical sense. "Are these experiences scientifically based?" I ask.

"Scientifically based?" Greyson thinks about that. "I do think that near-death experiences are scientifically based in that they follow rules and there's a constancy to them."

OK then, I persist: Were all these extraordinary journeys—the ones the psychiatrist has studied most of his life, the ones I have examined in this book—actual, real events?

Greyson waits awhile in silence. Then, "I don't know, I don't know."

After some pressing, he relents, however.

"Well, obviously their physical bodies didn't go through it. So the question is: Was that part of them that went through these experiences physical or not? The way we understand matter and energy now, I would say—it doesn't make sense to say they physically did it, that they physically went through their experiences.

"But I have to stress it's what we know now," he continues, "because what we know of matter is so little: We know only a small percent of all the matter in the universe. Because 80 percent of the universe is dark matter, which we cannot measure.

"And likewise, most of the energy of the universe is dark energy," Dr. Greyson continues. "It may be that when we do eventually understand what it's all about, that knowledge may also give us some understanding of what death experiences are all about."

By this the psychiatrist means that dark matter cannot be seen directly with telescopes because it doesn't emit or absorb light. It's composed primarily, cosmologists believe, of ghostly subatomic particles that can travel at the speed of light. They have no electrical charge, and generally physicists cannot see them. But scientists can see the wreckage one of these particles leaves behind when it strikes an atom: the pillaging of the ghost. So what Dr. Greyson is saying, and it is echoed by van Lommel and many others in the field, is that there's a whole mysterious dark universe within our more familiar world, one that we know almost nothing about. And within that dark universe there must be other realities.

"Because the out-of-body entity, the out-of-body experience: what is seen—it's not matter as we know matter,"

Dr. Greyson concludes. "It may be some kind of matter that we haven't understood yet."

It may well be: matter that we haven't yet understood, a universe within a universe. It is also undoubtedly something that we will understand some day. That is what is behind the operating room voyage of Pam Reynolds Lowery; the observations of the wise men in togas; the brilliant light, the extraordinary colors; the newfound ability to communicate without words, move through walls, and glimpse from on high the entire universe. That is why Gerry Rebach, enveloped in a golden bubble, saw the face of her dead friend without at the time realizing he was dead. That is just possibly what accounts for the travels.

Sam Parnia believes that the human ability to plumb and understand what goes on in death, in fact to insist on understanding, will expand exponentially, embracing and eventually cracking the mystery. The old questions—What is death? Why should death occur? What happens to us after death? What causes whatever happens to happen? What can we learn from it all?—will be answered. And answered soon.

"In our lifetime we will figure it out," he says firmly. "We will know what's happening."

And so until we do know everything, we must listen to those travelers who have ridden the wave of eternity, puzzled and awed. We already know an astonishing amount, thanks to experiencers and scientists, medical doctors and nurses—that the death we always imagined or feared or tried desperately to stave off isn't at all the sort of experience that awaits us. That something like pleasure and wisdom, adventure and surprise, beauty and delight can all come in death's wake. That once we've passed through, death can change us and the lives we choose to live.

Really, that's the one certainty. Death changes the living, almost always for the better. One of the last things Anthony Cicoria tells me is what death did to him: "At the time before I died, I was so focused, so narrow-minded and intent on this tunnel vision I had of where I was going and what I was doing," he says. "It seemed like after I was hit by lightning, not only did the purpose of my life change, but the things that became the primary focus changed. Prior to the lightning, I was really going down an academic path. I was publishing. I was really being groomed for a career as chairman of a university department. And I envisioned myself being there.

"But all that became . . ."—the surgeon searches for words but, finding none adequate to the job, shrugs heavily—"It really didn't matter anymore." By which he means that academic chairmanships, however desirable, took second place. Cicoria remarried his wife, Nina, about a month before I first met him. It's OK to hold different views about death travels from your spouse, he says now: That's what he's learned. Family, children—they are the important elements in life. As for death: "I guess I have some answers to questions that were burning in me ever since I can remember."

That is the nature of the River Styx of today. It not only encourages the boatman to ferry his passenger back to the shore of the living, but it also allows some of us the privilege of time to roam, at least for a while, through what once was the gated community of the dead, after which the visitor can return and remember.

It bathes us in perspective and comprehension. It lets the returned understand what does matter. Sooner or later, thanks to even more spectacular medical advances, Dr. Cicoria's travels, or some version of them, will likely be shared by more people than we can now imagine. Death voyages will be, in other words, more democratic, acceptable, credible, often glorious voyages of discovery.

"That's the key to the future," Dr. Parnia explains toward the end of our talk. "It's as though we are living in the 15th century, and there are all these undiscovered lands."

An amazing new world is what he means, just waiting for exploration.

CHAPTER NINE

GOING HOME

A SONGWRITER, a physician, an actress, a teacher, a student, a monk, a businesswoman, an artist, an engineer. Old or young, religious or irreligious—they are all united by three distinct elements: They died, they returned from the dead, and they returned with vivid recollections of their experiences while dead. Each experience was distinctive to the individual, each etched for years thereafter in the minds of those who returned to life, affecting every portion of existence: their actions, their livelihoods, their marriages, their choice of friends. Most saw a brilliant light. Most met bliss when bliss might be least expected. In death, they found themselves in any number of surprise scenarios: either alone or among intriguing strangers, released in hospital rooms from their own useless bodies or soaring among planets and stars, communing with dead relatives or, alternatively, communing with their own inner selves.

And then they crossed back over the border, returning to life, usually with tremendous reluctance. And on those occasions when they summon the nerve to speak about their recollections, they generally run into an iron fence of disbelief and derision, and not only from spouses or friends. From orthodox scientists as well—the very people trained to examine and investigate the phenomena of our world.

To be perfectly honest, until about three years ago, I wouldn't have believed those travelers either. I may not have said it out loud, but my silent response would have been: *You were hallucinating . . . oxygen deprived . . . feverish. . . . You weren't really dead. . . . You need to see a shrink. Badly. Today.*

But by now I have spent years of my life knocking on the doors of strangers and speaking to the very people whose accounts I was once prone to dismiss—maybe even anxious to dismiss, because I knew that accepting their versions of their own realities would require a thorough and lengthy reevaluation of everything I had previously believed. Reevaluating what constitutes death, as it turns out, takes time and a tremendous amount of effort. And of course at the end of all that effort at comprehension, at the end of revising a good deal of what I previously believed, after listening to the revelations of all these travelers, I am still left wondering. For every question answered—yes, these individuals were sentient and alert even when dead; yes, they were still themselves while deceased but actually *themselves plus*, equipped with surprising new abilities—a million more questions crop up. Among the most important: *Why were these people selected to go on these voyages? Will we all do the same when we die?*

And after considerable examination, a lot of thought, and many interviews with the once dead and those scientists and doctors who have studied their recollections and on occasion the brains and bodies of those who died and returned, I think the answer to those questions is: Yes, I suspect we will all go on some sort of trip when our time comes. The people I've met and spoken to were not selected because they were particularly unusual; they were not fantasists or habitual liars, desperate for attention. They were pretty much like most people: hardworking, intelligent, questioning, and on occasion—before their unexpected journeys—skeptical. So I figure their fascinating death experiences—although startling and even perhaps initially improbable to us, the living—are probably, as we will all likely find out, pretty commonplace as well.

For one reason or another, those I spoke to just happened to recall what happened to them after crossing the border. There may be reasons why they have vivid memories when others returning from the dead do not: Perhaps they received better and quicker resuscitation. Or maybe, as Dr. Parnia has hypothesized, those with recollections of their journeys did not suffer inflammation or swelling of the brain, which can damage memory.

I have to be honest here: Initially, I wasn't really eager to attend conferences held by death travelers or go to meetings at which they recounted their adventures, accounts often accompanied by tears. I had a feeling (one that turned out to be baseless) that I'd be drowning for hours in the babble of the delusional and the self-absorbed. In other words, I thought time spent with vast groups of these people a complete waste of time in my quest for answers. There simply had to be, I was certain, some hard scientific evidence—something I would inevitably discover during my research—that would answer the *how* and *why* of these reported death experiences.

But what I learned very early in my investigation is that despite all the valiant efforts of the Galileos to discover what lies behind these voyages, there aren't any definite answers at all from science.

Scientists can guess at certain possibilities, make a few stabs at explaining why the returning dead report a brilliant light or a surprise death encounter. But these are just that: guesses. They cannot tell us why a completely anesthetized Pam Reynolds Lowery, her eyes taped shut and her ears blocked, could describe with perfect accuracy the look and sound of an intricate medical instrument or the anxious conversations of the medical staff when her femoral artery proved too small. They cannot as yet give a good explanation for why Anthony Cicoria, lying prostrate on the ground after being struck by lightning, had somehow or other seen his children having their faces painted at that very moment. The work of the Galileos, which might provide the world with some answers, perhaps comforting and exciting answers about what happens after we die, is generally either underfunded or else simply and without apology ignored.

Which is what made a 2013 decision by the University of California, Riverside, to provide support, moral and financial, for investigations into these death travels so spectacular—a kind of miracle, really. "I've got some great news to tell you!" a jubilant Dr. Greyson said to me soon thereafter. As it turned out, Dr. Parnia, with whom Greyson occasionally collaborates, had just received a $240,000 grant from the academic institution to continue his and Greyson's out-of-body research among heart attack patients. Titled "A Multi-Centre Pilot Study of the Mind, Brain, Consciousness and Near Death Experiences during Cardiac Arrest," the funded study was actually more significant than a miracle. It was an act of faith, and a rare one. One thing is certain: It is an invaluable start to legitimizing and examining what can no longer be ignored.

Because the intricacy of these voyages and their long-term aftereffects on those who return to life do need far more serious investigation. All of the previously dead, every one of them I've interviewed, found in death what Dr. Parnia calls "these undiscovered lands." And all of them, even those who were initially wary or frightened on their journeys, returning puzzled and unhappy, ultimately found themselves grateful for that gift of discovery. They know what most of us do not know—not yet, anyway: Death is not the end. That is what every last one of them says, and frankly, I believe them. We don't know—yet—how long these death voyages last. It could be for a few hours or it could be, as Dr. van Lommel strongly believes, that it lasts an eternity. But right now his conviction is just that: a belief.

This we do know, however: Delightful or distressing, something extraordinary is going on after life. The very fact that this something exists, that it is an indelible memory in those who return from the dead, and subsequently a force that exerts a profound influence on the rest of their lives, should tell us a lot. Our minds will not vanish. We will be, for at least a while, maybe forever, curiously empowered in ways we never were while alive. We will be enveloped, at least for a time, by comprehension. This is our future.

My mother would not have believed any of this. Time and again, she had made that much clear to me—and of course by the time she was drowning in dementia, there wasn't much point in explaining what I had learned. There were nonetheless a few surprise moments, some of them heralded by Dr. Greyson. Toward the very end, despite the Alzheimer's, my mother suddenly recognized my youngest son. And she was under no illusions, for some reason, about what was soon to happen.

"You're scared of death, aren't you?" I ventured.

A vigorous nod. She knew what I was saying.

I knew by then that death was nothing to be scared of. That something else was on the horizon. But I also began to recognize that my frequent visits to my declining mother were helping to keep her alive: I was the buffer between life and death, and it is not a good thing to be when you know someone you love badly needs to cross the border—to go home. Especially when you know that beyond that, within that home, there might be some illumination, something big and important. I had heard a few hospice nurses tell helpless relatives who watched their loved ones suffer to leave the room: That way the terminal patient gets permission to die. And very often the patient does in fact die in such circumstances.

In mid-August 2013, I decided in my own way to leave the room. The French cologne I had often dabbed on my mother's neck and forehead lay for the first time untouched in its bottle. Gazing at her, I thought of Bill Taylor, who had, like the great psychoanalyst Carl Jung, glimpsed the universe while dead.

I loved those adventures, the luminous sights. I thought they were something to look forward to, even though I doubted my mother, a very practical person, much grounded in the day-to-day, would share that particular experience. It's not her sort of death, and I think if I've learned one thing about death voyages, it's that they are as varied and distinctive as the individuals who journey. Although with my mother, who knows? She always loved to travel.

I switched on a Bach concerto for her benefit. When I looked up, there at the foot of her bed stood Gerry Rebach, the hospice nurse I had interviewed eight months before. We hadn't seen each other since the day she had told me about being enveloped in a golden bubble of peace while she glimpsed the image of a close friend—a friend who turned out to have just died.

"Small world," Gerry said, hugging me. Then she seemed to vanish. She was not my mother's hospice nurse, and she had other patients to care for.

When she left, I took my mother's hand, which was wasted, the veins smaller than ever and by now a very light blue. I said a silent goodbye. Then I went home to pack. That evening I flew to the Netherlands.

Two days later, at 9 a.m. on August 12, 2013, it was Gerry Rebach who appeared by my mother's bedside. She just happened to be passing by. It was also she who told my husband that my mother had died right then, just as he walked into her room.

At that moment it was 3 p.m. in the Netherlands, and I was interviewing Pim van Lommel. From my purse I heard the ping of my cell phone. And I knew without a glance exactly what had happened. But if I had rummaged through my purse and checked to make sure, I would have had to interrupt Dr. van Lommel and explain that my mother had just died, and I really didn't want to. I wanted to continue in the realm of thought and consciousness and experience after death. I hoped my mother was having all of that, that her real mind, the one I used to know, was at last free to think.

So the interview continued.

"What made you decide to write this book?" asked Dr. van Lommel at the end of our talk.

I used to work as a volunteer in a hospice, I told him. I've thought a lot about death and what happens afterward. I used to be so fearful, so unhappy about it. Now I'm really quite different.

He didn't seem satisfied. "A number of people who work in hospices have had near-death experiences," he said, treading lightly.

"Not me, not yet," I assured him. "But it's amazing, now that I'm researching and writing the book, how many friends tell me they've either had a death experience or that they know someone who's had one, and then I'm introduced, and sure enough, I hear yet another account. People I've known for ages and ages, who've never mentioned any of this before. Then I call them, and they start talking."

"Ahhh . . . ," said the cardiologist. "It's always like that."

ACKNOWLEDGMENTS

FOR RICHARD THE AGNOSTIC, who put aside everything, including his nonbeliefs and his free time, and helped guide me through Georgia, Delaware, Maryland, Virginia, Britain, the Netherlands, New York, Arizona, Pennsylvania, Washington, D.C., and also the bright places neither of us knows firsthand.

For Tim Cox and the remarkable nurses, doctors, chaplain, and volunteers at the Washington Home and Community Hospices, all of whom helped first me—and then my mother—through passages of light, understanding, and grief. I owe all of you more than I can ever repay.

For Karl A. Greene—thank you for looking over the technical aspects of Pam Reynolds Lowery's operation, in which you participated.

For the doctors who are scorned by their colleagues, and the nurses whose reports are dismissed by the doctors, and the professors who are refused tenure, and the scientists whose research and results are disregarded and unfunded.

And for the travelers. Thank you for leading the way, even if it was a very lonely way for a very long time.

NOTES

Chapter 1. *The Light Is What Happens*

1. One of the television crews who filmed Pam Reynolds Lowery, a British crew, thought the same. In fact, they asked an astonished Dr. Greene, "Do you really think she's all there? Do you think she's sane?" Dr. Greene is decided in his opinion: "I thought she was perfectly sane," he tells me. "And I told the television crew the same."

Chapter 3. *What Are Death Experiences?*

1. Greyson isn't the only researcher to categorize the various elements of a death experience; Raymond Moody did so before him in his 1975 book, *Life After Life*. But Greyson's is the more modern, carefully assembled version.

2. Bruce Greyson, "Near-Death Encounters With and Without Near-Death Experiences: Comparative NDE Scale Profiles," *Journal of Near-Death Studies* 8, no. 3 (Spring 1990).

3. Sam Parnia, *What Happens When We Die: A Ground-breaking Study Into the Nature of Life and Death*. New York: Hay House, 2007.

4. Pim van Lommel et al., "Near-Death Experience in Survivors of Cardiac Arrest: A Prospective Study in the Netherlands," *The Lancet* 358, no. 9298 (December 15, 2001). The cardiac patient also told the nurse that as a result of his experience, he was no longer afraid of death.

5. Although modern CPR was first demonstrated experimentally in the 1950s, it wasn't a widely promoted technique until later. It is—and is not—an entirely new procedure. In its hit-or-miss form, it has been around since the 18th century; at that time, bellows were sometimes used to help drowning victims breathe, and bloodletting was also included in the procedure. By the 1960s, a vastly improved form of CPR was promoted by the American Red Cross, incorporating chest compressions and mouth-to-mouth resuscitation. By the 1990s, publicly available defibrillators could be found at airports, schools, and other public places.

6. For 10 to 20 percent to return with death memories is, I realize, a fairly wide bridge. And readers of Chapter 2 will note yet another variation on the number of death travelers. The percentage depends entirely on the study completed. Some studies report 5 percent, others 15 percent or 18 percent, and still others 20 percent. In this instance, I am using the statistics cited by Dr. Bruce Greyson, the psychiatrist who heads the University of Virginia's Division of

Perceptual Studies and who has made a lifetime study of these experiences.

7. In 1976, Colonel Corcoran's father had the same sort of experience following a heart attack. "He said he felt himself come out of his body; he looked around then went someplace beautiful," she recalls him telling her. "And he was totally bewildered because he didn't believe in any of these things. He couldn't come to grips with it. He said, 'I know this happened to me, I know this is real. But I still don't want to talk about it anymore.' And I thought to myself, *Oh my God, if he could tell me about this, then this is something we have to get on top of.*"

8. Neurosurgeon Wilder Penfield discovered this—in fact, in 1934, during temporal lobe surgery, a patient informed Penfield she was reliving an earlier experience in her life. Wilder Penfield, M.D., "The Twenty-Ninth Maudsley Lecture: The Role of the Temporal Cortex in Certain Psychical Phenomena," *Journal of Mental Science* 101, no. 424 (July 1955).

Chapter 4. Bliss

1. One of the biggest difficulties in recounting a death voyage, as any experiencer will tell you, is that much of what he has seen or learned is indescribable and almost invariably inexplicable. That's why you learn that connecting planetary threads, say, are composed of energy or love. Or that the individual is for a time a radio receiver with no thoughts of her own, just thoughts that are somehow transmitted to her.

The experiences don't always transmute into language. In fact, they almost never do.

2. Moorjani's book, *Dying to Be Me* (2012), explains her journey in greater detail. In it, she writes that her lymphoma receded to nothingness in the weeks and months after she awoke from her coma. Hers is the one instance in this book that is actually near death—that is, no clinical death occurred, although her coma lasted 30 hours.

3. I thought Bill Taylor's vision of the beautiful universe unique, almost absurdly improbable, until I read Dr. Jung's own vibrant account. But as it turns out, neither man's experience was exactly rare. Around 29 percent of the Dutch cardiac patients who returned from death with memories they reported to van Lommel and his colleagues said that during clinical death they had seen a "celestial landscape."

4. Readers who might wonder why quite a number of death experiences occur during labor and childbirth—two are mentioned in this book and I've interviewed three women who experienced death during childbirth, which might seem an unusually high number of fatalities—should know that it is far more dangerous a procedure than we are currently led to believe in popular literature. Just a century ago, "what to expect when you're expecting" used to be—quite possibly—death. Indeed, before the advent of modern medicine and sterilized surgical tools, maternal mortality was, especially in the event of complications, sometimes the anticipated by-product of giving birth: By one estimate, 1.5 out of every 100 women died giving birth

between 1700 and 1750 in those English parishes that kept records. By 1850, 1 out of every 200 women died giving birth, according to similar parish records, referenced by the *Journal of the Royal Society of Medicine* (November 2006).

5. Also known as tetrachloroethylene. Short-term exposure can cause irritation of the throat as well as the central nervous system. Exposure to heavy vapors, frequently administered, can cause death.

6. External cardiac massage is performed when there is no pulse felt in the neck or the groin.

7. Years later, Jayne Smith told the NDE pioneer Raymond Moody about her husband's response when she asked him if he'd inquired about what went exactly wrong during labor. Moody told her, "Jayne, I understand that. I wouldn't want anyone telling me my wife had died and my child had almost died. No, thank you! Just tell me everyone's fine."

8. Neuropsychiatrist Peter Fenwick reports the following from a retrospective NDE study of 450 participants: "I was particularly interested in the pastoral landscapes because they are also reported by terminally ill patients in approaching-death experiences. The landscapes have always been described as very beautiful and usually include wonderful flowers." There were even botanists in his NDE study, but they reported when they returned to life, Dr. Fenwick observes, "no new species, only species they already knew." Peter Fenwick, M.D., F.R.C.Psych., "Science and Spirituality: A Challenge for the 21st Century," Bruce Greyson Lecture, Annual Conference,

International Association for Near-Death Studies, 2004. Jayne Smith is remarkable because her death landscape seems to be composed of new floral species bearing colors she had never before seen and that don't exist in life.

9. Epilepsy seizures are not, as certain misguided assumptions would have it, benign events. Epilepsy more than doubles the risk of dying, according to the Epilepsy Foundation, and back-to-back seizures, the long kind Charlotte Rohrer experienced, can be fatal and need immediate emergency medical care.

Chapter 5. Hell or Something Like It

1. After tonic-clonic seizures, the kind that afflict Charlotte Rohrer, epilepsy sufferers usually remember nothing at all. Neuropsychiatrist Dr. Fenwick is insistent on this score. "Seizures are always destructive, the minute you get a seizure you would never get anything like a near-death experience," he says. Those who insist a memory of a death experience must have been caused by a seizure are, he says, "all imagining things. I've dealt with epilepsy all my life. It's all imaginings by people who are looking in the wrong place for an explanation." Author's note: Both my adult children also have epilepsy, the kind in fact from which Charlotte Rohrer suffers. Since adolescence, they've experienced tonic-clonic seizures leading to unconsciousness, after which—I have naturally interviewed them both on this subject—they remember nothing at all. Not a thing. After lesser, fully conscious seizures involving, say,

a simple jerking of the arm or legs, they do recall incidents: lying on a bed, breaking a plate, shaking. But these are events the rest of us who are seizure-free have observed as well.

2. Bruce Greyson and Nancy Evans Bush, "Distressing Near-Death Experiences," *Psychiatry* 55 (February 1992): 95–110.

3. Greyson points specifically to one variety of bad death experience where the individual is left with "a pervasive sense of emptiness and fatalistic despair after the event." There are other varieties, however: "the 'hellish' experience, as well as an experience—much like Charlotte Rohrer's—that may start off as pleasant," similar to most experiences, but which, Greyson notes, is ultimately "interpreted as terrifying."

4. Nancy eventually divorced her husband; he is now deceased.

5. For years, Nancy tells me, she had told people, "I really don't know whether I died or not that day in the hospital." All she knew was something really bad had happened during childbirth. Then she analyzed bit by bit what happened sequentially: the flight above the hospital roof, the soaring over the Hudson River, the bleak travel through the stone-gray universe. "I actually left Earth," she realized, stricken. Like Jung after his heart attack. "I died," she concluded.

Chapter 6. Those We Meet

1. From *Memories, Dreams, Reflections*, written in 1957 when the great psychoanalyst was 81 years old. "There was something of the genius about him," Jung wrote about his doctor.

2. Readers can find most of what Jung recollected after recovery from his heart attack here: www.near-death.com/jung.html.

3. Agonal breathing usually occurs shortly before a patient's death. It is loud and labored and can precede what is known as the death rattle. However, agonal respirations can also persist for a few minutes after a heart ceases beating.

4. The following day, says James, Helen died for good.

5. It is interesting to note that Fenwick and Greyson observed significantly different proportions of experiencers who had encountered spiritual beings on their journey.

6. Zodiacs are often used in military operations.

7. This is not at all surprising. As the researcher Cherie Sutherland found, when death travelers try to discuss their journeys, half of all the relatives in whom they confide reject their account, as do 25 percent of their friends and 85 percent of their doctors. Nurses tend to be more accepting: Only 30 percent reject these accounts, Sutherland points out.

8. This is also reported by Sutherland.

Chapter 7. With or Without God

1. In this instance, I used the term "near-death experience" because, as mentioned, it is the classical phrase, and everyone in hospice would immediately understand it. Also, hospice patients really *are* near death.

2. Dr. Siegel refers to his dying body as "he" because the real person, he believes, was hovering over that body.

3. Just 3 percent of children, Atwater also discovered, have a nasty or hellish experience.

4. Pim van Lommel, *Consciousness Beyond Life: The Science of the Near-Death Experience*, 2011.

Chapter 8. Unasked-For Gifts: The Knowing and the Powers

1. However, neuropsychiatrist Peter Fenwick is also quick to add: "I'd also point out that heightened sensitivity, a proclaimed ability to read minds, can also occur after a head injury as well. Cerebral damage can cause this."

2. From Pim van Lommel, *Consciousness Beyond Life*.

3. As Richard Alpert, Ram Dass was part of the Harvard University psychology department. It was there that he gained some notoriety for his work with the psychedelic guru Timothy Leary. He was, like Leary, ultimately dismissed from Harvard. In 1997 Ram Dass experienced a stroke. Jayne Smith's account dates from the 1980s.

ABOUT THE AUTHOR

A LONGTIME JOURNALIST and contributing editor to *Vanity Fair,* Judy Bachrach writes political, social, and arts commentaries for print and online publications around the world. In 2008 she founded The Checkout Line, the first online advice column for the terminally ill and their loved ones. Her first book, *Tina and Harry Come to America* (Free Press, 2001), was a biography of magazine editor Tina Brown and her husband, Harry Evans. Bachrach lives in Washington, D.C., and regularly teaches journalism at John Cabot University in Rome, Italy.